CROSS-COUNTRY SKI TRAILS

of
Washington's Cascades
and Olympics

CROSS-COUNTRY SKI TRAILS

of
Washington's Cascades and Olympics

Tom Kirkendall and Vicky Spring

The Mountaineers/Seattle

The Mountaineers: Organized 1906
". . . to explore, study, preserve and enjoy
the natural beauty of the Northwest."

First edition; first printing October 1983, second printing January 1984,
third printing September 1984, fourth printing January 1985

Published by
The Mountaineers
306 2nd Ave. W., Seattle, WA 98119

Published simultaneously in Canada by
Douglas & McIntyre Ltd.
1615 Venables St.
Vancouver, B.C. V5L 2H1

Manufactured in the United States of America

Edited by Harvey Manning
Copyedited by Tricia Silver
Designed by Marge Mueller
Maps by John Sherman

Photos on pages 10, 12, 22, 34, 42, 43, 53, 62, 66, 76, 81, 84, 111, 124, 126, 129,
132, 139, 144, 160, 167, 183, 199 by Bob and Ira Spring
Cover photo: Lake Wenatchee and Dirtyface Peak (Trail 33).

Library of Congress Cataloguing in Publication Data
Kirkendall, Tom.
    Cross-country ski trails of Washington's Cascades and Olympics.
    Bibliography: p.
    Includes index.
    1. Cross-country skiing—Washington (State)—Olympic Mountains—Guide-
books. 2. Cross-country skiing—Cascade Range—Guide-books. 3. Olympic
Mountains (Wash.)—Description. 4. Cascade Range—Description. I. Spring,
Vicky, 1953-   . II. Title. GV854.5.W33K57 1983   917.97′5   83-13488
ISBN 0-89886-062-8

09876

Skier at Paradise, Mt. Rainier National Park

To the Kirkendalls, Ben and Mary,
our heart-felt thanks for their support
and enthusiasm.

To the Springs, our great appreciation
for Pat's cheerful typing and unofficial editing
and Honorable Father's help and suggestions.

CONTENTS

Preface 11

Introduction 13

NOOKSACK RIVER
1 Mt. Baker Trail 24
2 Canyon Creek Road 26
3 Wells Creek 29
4 North Fork
  Nooksack River Road 31
5 Artist Point 33
6 Herman Saddle 35

BAKER RIVER
7 Park Butte 36
8 Martin Lake
  —Morovitz Loop 39

SKAGIT RIVER
9 Finney Creek Road 41

METHOW RIVER
10 Castle Ranch Loop 43
11 Diamond T Ranch
   —Rendevous Pass 46
12 Buck Mountain Loop 48
13 Pipestone Canyon 50
14 Sun Mountain 52
15 Methow Valley Trail 54
16 Loup-Loup 56
17 Telemark Mountain 58

SUIATTLE RIVER
18 Green Mountain 60

DARRINGTON
19 North Mountain 63
20 Segelsen Creek Road 64

SOUTH FORK
STILLAGUAMISH RIVER
21 Pilchuck Mountain
   Road 67
22 Deer Creek Road 70
23 Double Eagle Road 72
24 Big Four Picnic Area 73
25 Coal Lake 75

SKYKOMISH RIVER
26 Miller River 77
27 Foss River 79
28 Beckler Peak Road 82
29 Heather Ridge 84

NASON CREEK
30 Mill Creek 87
31 Coulter Ski Trail 88
32 Chiwaukum Mountains
   (Scottish Lakes) 90

LAKE WENATCHEE
33 Lake Wenatchee State Park 93
34 White River Viewpoint . . .95
35 Flying Loop 97

LEAVENWORTH
36 Leavenworth 99

MIDDLE FORK
SNOQUALMIE RIVER
37 Bessemer Mountain 102

SOUTH FORK
SNOQUALMIE RIVER
38 Bandera Overlook 104
39 Hansen Creek 106

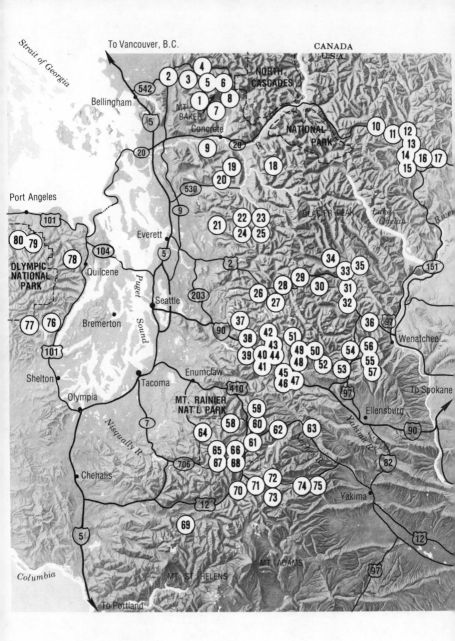

KEECHELUS LAKE

40	Cold Creek	108
41	Three Forks Trails	110
42	Kendall Peak Road	112
43	Gold Creek Valley	115
44	Mt. Margaret	117
45	Amabilis Mountain	120

46	Cabin Creek	122
47	South Kachess Lake	124

CLE ELUM LAKE

48	French Cabin Creek	126
49	Cle Elum River	128

50 Jolly and Jolly Too 131
51 Cooper River Road 132

SWAUK CREEK
52 Teanaway Butte 134
53 Red Top Mountain
   Lookover 136
54 Blewett Pass 138
55 Swauk Pass
   Meadow Loops 141
56 Wenatchee Ridge 143
57 Haney Meadow 144

WHITE RIVER
58 Grand Park 146
59 Bullion Basin 148
60 Silver Basin 150
61 Chinook Pass
   and Naches Peak 152

AMERICAN RIVER
62 Pleasant Valley Loop 154

NACHES RIVER
63 Rocky Prairie 156

MT. RAINIER
64 Mowich Lake 159

65 Reflection Lakes 161
66 Tatoosh Range 163
67 Mazama Ridge 165
68 Camp Muir 167

COWLITZ RIVER
69 Burley Mountain 170
70 Packwood Lake 172
71 Yellow Jacket Road 174
72 Hogback Mountain 177
73 Sand Lake 178

TIETON RIVER
74 Goose Egg Trail 181
75 Lost Lake 183

OLYMPICS
76 Big Creek Road 185
77 Four Stream Road 187
78 Mt. Townsend 190
79 Obstruction Point 192
80 Hurricane Hill 194

And More Ski Trails 196

Suggested Reading 203

Index 204

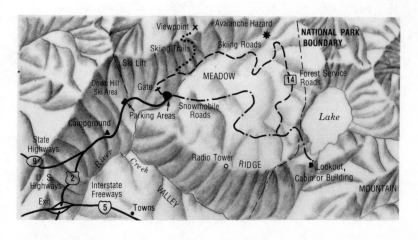

Winter wonderland

PREFACE

WINTER WONDERLAND?

The Winter Wonderland—where has it gone? Whatever happened to the vast quiet of snow time, the great peace beyond the racket of contraptions, the escape from machinery into a land where the fastest thing going was a rabbit?

—Well, the ski mountaineer still can find it, but he may have to climb halfway up a cliff or all the way to the top of a volcano to be free from the racket of snowmobiles. As for the Nordic skier, he can learn to put up with the snarl of speeding snow machines—or he can start complaining to the Forest Service, demanding a fair share of the winter.

Let's face it—the snowmobile is a road gobbler. A Nordic skier going 2 to 3 miles an hour needs only 5 to 10 miles of space for a day's recreation, and the only creatures that hear him coming are the local rabbits. A snowmobiler racing 30 to 50 miles an hour needs 50 to 150 miles of space for *his* day, and you can hear him miles away—a lucky thing too, or you might not have time to duck.

Because snowmobilers are well organized and well financed by the industry and because they pay license fees and a gas tax, they get respect from the Forest Service, which receives money to develop snowmobile areas above and beyond fees and taxes and thus gains a vested bureaucratic interest in the industry. To be fair it must be said that the Forest Service would be happy to develop areas for cross-country skiing if somebody would pay them to do the job. However, Nordic skiers are a poor bunch to look to for money. A tax on skis would hardly be equitable since some folks use their skis twice in a lifetime, others nine months in the year—and some have such terrible luck they need three pairs of skis to get through a season.

Actually, the problem is not of the sort that requires money. Cross-country skiers don't need to be coddled. Groomed trails are very nice, but most Nordic skiers are fully content with any old logging road. They merely ask that it be a *quiet* road and that snowmobiles not make it too icy and rutted for skis. The difficulty is that the very roads best suited for quiet gliding, especially by the beginning skier, are precisely those best for high-speed racketing.

However, just because they have more money and make more noise (political, too), do snowmobilers have the right to grab all the land they want? Skiers (and their quiet brethren, the snowshoers) constitute far more than half the winter recreationists. Don't they deserve at least half of the winter? The money argument doesn't stand up; it wouldn't cost the Forest Service a fortune to nail up a few signs—at $10 apiece— designating certain roads as solely for self-propelled sports and to indicate these roads on the maps they hand out to snowmobilers.

Young skier marvels at the fresh, new world after a winter snow storm

Every time the Forest Service opens a road to snowmobiles, it should set aside an equally scenic road, of the same length in the same area, for skiers and snowshoers.

The Forest Service knows in its heart what it *should* be doing. The Monte Cristo Ranger District has three beautiful view roads set aside for self-propelled sports. —But the other six roads in the district are for snowmobiles! Some districts are marking, or even packing, loops of a mile or two in the forest, but these efforts miss the point. Most people want to ski or snowshoe to a viewpoint, a lake, or some other scenic destination. Moreover, they want to do so free from the racket, stink, danger, and tracks of machines.

If Nordic skiers ever expect to get justice, they're going to have to start making more noise—not in the wilderness—in the cities. They must first write repeated letters to the Forest Service Ranger districts and Front Headquarters, requesting that a fair share of roads be returned to the Winter Wonderland. They must also join outdoor organizations, such as The Mountaineers, and work with them to put the same pressure on the Forest Service as is done by the snowmobile industry.

INTRODUCTION

Every year more and more people head into the woods on "skinny skis." Many are reformed downhillers fleeing from high prices, long lift lines, packed runs, and yodeling on the loudspeaker. Others are ski mountaineers seeking a less strenuous way to spend the winter. Some never have skied at all because neither of the other two forms of the sport appealed to them. Nordic, or cross-country, skiing is something completely different. Anyone can enjoy it — except, perhaps, people who absolutely despise snow.

Washington's Cascade and Olympic Mountains provide infinite opportunity for excellent Nordic skiing, whether on groomed trails along peaceful valley foors, scenic logging roads, or open slopes of dormant volcanoes that cry out to be telemarked. This book can only begin to suggest how much there is to do and in how many areas. Particular emphasis has been given the needs of the beginning (basic) and intermediate skier who is just learning the country, but trails and routes have been included that will test the advanced and challenge the mountaineer.

To repeat the caution that any guidebook must offer — especially one that deals in so undependable a substance as snow — the reader must keep in mind the publication date of this book. If he skis onto the scene a couple years later, he must understand that the authors have no control over (1) the building of new roads or washing out of old ones, (2) the rules and regulations of government agencies, and (3) the falling down of trees and the piling up (or not piling up) of snow. In a word: Conditions are never the same twice, so be flexible in your plans.

GUIDE TO THE GUIDEBOOK

Skill Level

Each of the trails has been classified by the skill required for an enjoyable trip. For the sake of simplicity we have used four levels that are broad and somewhat overlapping; consider them to be merely suggestions.

Basic: No skill requirement. Anyone can have fun the very first time on skis. These trails generally are in open meadows, valley bottoms, or on quite flat logging roads.

Intermediate: The minimum skills required are traverse; herringbone; kick-turn; and simple stopping techniques such as pole-dragging, snowplow, sitting down; and a good sense of humor. These trails generally are logging roads or marked Forest Service loops.

Advanced: The minimum skills required are full control of skis at all times, telemark (or any turn), and quick stops. Some advanced trails require basic routefinding. Trails at this level include steep and narrow logging roads, summer hiking trails, and overland routes.

Mountaineer: The minimum skills required in addition to an advanced skill level are competence in routefinding and knowledge of snow and avalanche conditions, weather, winter camping, winter survival, and mountaineering.

Trip Length (X miles to a scenic place)

Snow levels vary from year to year and from day to day and therefore the starting point, especially on logging roads, may vary. A base point (which may or may not be your actual starting point) has been assigned; the trailhead elevation and skiing time are figured from this point.

Skiing Time

This is the time spent traveling to and from the destination and does not include lunch or rest stops. The times are calculated from the trail's base point. If the snowline is above this point, plan less time; if below, plan more. The times given for each trail assume good conditions. If a track must be broken through heavy snow or the surface is extremely hard ice, add a generous amount of extra time.

Variable Miles and Times

In some cases the number of miles and amount of skiing time given are variable. These trails are generally over logging roads where snow level suggests different starting points and destinations in winter and spring.

Best Skiing Time

If you want to know what an "average" snow year is in Washington's Cascade or Olympic Mountains, don't ask a seasoned skier; all you'll get is a year-by-year description of the differences. There never is, in real life, an "average" winter. Some years skiing must be done at 5000 feet or above; other years skiing is good through June at 3000 feet; some years the skiing is superb on Seattle's golf courses for most of January.

In an attempt to say when skiing is best for each trail, certain generalizations have been made about that mythical average snow year. The time band given is a narrow one. Skiing often starts as much as a month before given times and lasts a month after. Some winters skiing may not be possible on trails below 4000 to 5000 feet. If in doubt, call the area ranger station, listen to pass reports, or contact local mountain shops before starting out.

Avalanche Potential

Trails in this book have been selected for their safety in winter and no known areas of extreme hazard have been included. The warnings given here are about areas to avoid at times when the snow is unstable. To know what these times are, skiers must make it their responsibility to in-

Mt. Shuksan from Artist Point—Trail 5

form themselves about current weather and snow conditions. For up-to-date information on the Washington Cascades and Olympics call (206) 285-WASH. For Snoqualmie Pass call (206) 442-SNOW. For specific trails call the ranger station in that district; on weekends there will be a recorded message.

Your best defense against avalanches is knowledge. Check the "Suggested Reading List" for detailed discussions. Several things to particularly watch for:

• Avalanche danger is especially high during *warming trends or after a heavy snowfall*; at these times avoid leeward slopes and travel on ridge tops.

• Steep hillsides, particularly north-facing, receive their first dose of sun for many months in the spring. After being stable all winter, these slopes may be covered by *spring*, or *climax, avalanches.*

• Wind causes snow to build up on the leeward side of ridges, creating dangerous overhangs called *cornices*. Use caution when approaching a ridge top—you may walk out atop a cornice with empty air beneath. A good rule is never to ski beyond the line of trees or snowblown rocks that mark the true crest of a ridge. It is equally dangerous to ski under a cornice as over it. Cornices may break off and trigger avalanches below.

Forecasting agencies express the daily hazard in the following four classifications:

1. Low Avalanche Hazard—mostly stable snow.
2. Moderate Avalanche Hazard—areas of unstable snow on steep, open slopes or gullies.
3. High Avalanche Hazard—snow pack very unstable. Avalanches highly probable on steep slopes and in gullies.
4. Extreme Avalanche Hazard—travel in the mountains unsafe. Better to head for the beach.

These classifications of *hazard* have to do with the *weather's* contribution to the avalanches. Each trail in this book has been rated as to the *potential* of the *terrain* for avalanches. The two factors of hazard and potential must be put together by the skier to make an accurate judgment of the situation.

If the avalanche potential for the trail is listed as *none*, the trail may be safely skied on days when the hazard is low, moderate, or high.

Areas with *low* avalanche potential normally may be skied on days when the hazard is low or moderate.

A *moderate* avalanche potential indicates the area is always to be skied with caution and then only when the hazard is low.

Avalanche forecasting is not an exact science. As when driving a car, one has to accept a certain amount of risk and use the forecast as a guide, not as a certainty. It is important always to seek up-to-date avalanche information before each trip even for trips of low to moderate avalanche potential.

Maps

Blankets of snow add new difficulties to routefinding. Signs are covered, road junctions are obscured, and trails blend into the surrounding countryside. Never start out without a good map of the area to be skied.

Each trail description lists the topographic maps for the trip. These maps are published by the U.S. Geological Survey (USGS) and can be purchased at outdoor equipment stores, map stores, or by writing the U.S. Geological Survey, Federal Center, Denver, Colorado 80225.

While USGS maps are the best for studying the works of nature, such as cliffs and rivers, they are not revised often enough to be current on the works of man, such as roads and clearcuts. When skiing logging roads, also carry a Green Trails map, available at outdoor equipment stores, or an up-to-date Forest Service map obtainable for a small fee at ranger stations (on weekdays) or by writing the district offices.

Skiers at commercial resorts are protected from avalanche hazards; cross-country skiers must rely on their own knowledge and judgment

Camp Robbers impatiently waiting for a share of lunch

Sno-Parks

Sno-Parks are designated winter parking areas plowed throughout the winter for recreationists. Permits are required to park in these areas and the fees provide funds to keep the parking sites open. Cars parking without permits can count on a ticket and possible towing.

Permits are available at outdoor equipment stores or by mail from:

Office of Winter Recreation
Washington State Parks and Recreation Commission
7150 Cleanwater Lane KY-11
Olympia, Washington 98505
Phone: (206) 754-1253

Snow-Play Areas

As the name suggests, these are areas to enjoy the snow by walking, sledding, snowshoeing, skiing, or any other nonmotorized activity. They are great for families and are usually located only a short way from the car. A few require a Sno-Park permit, but most are plowed out by the Forest Service. For specific location contact a ranger station.

HEADING OUT INTO WINTER

This book doesn't explain *how* to ski, just *where*. However, some tips may be offered to help orient skiers toward wintertime fun. Further information can be found in the books listed in the back.

Technique

Cross-country skiing looks simple enough but proper technique is very important to insure a good time. Even expert downhillers have problems the first day on skinny skis. The narrowness, flexible bindings, and low shoes give an entirely different feeling. Books are helpful, but one or two lessons may be needed. Many organizations offer a two-lesson plan, the first to get you started in the right direction and the second, a month later to correct any problems you may have.

Clothing

There is no dress code for cross-country skiing. Clothing can be anything from high fashion to mismatched Army surplus. Many of the garments sold for cross-country are designed for resort skiing or racing and provide flexibility and style, but not much warmth.

In the wilderness, warmth is crucial. Covering your body from head to toe in wool, using two or more layers on the upper body to regulate heating, insures a pleasant journey rather than a bone-chilling ordeal.

Rain gear is essential. Ponchos keep snow and rain off of a person who is standing still, but can be somewhat awkward when one is skiing. Rain pants and jackets made of coated nylon or breathable waterproof material work best for warmth, dryness, and flexibility.

Skis and Boots

What length skis to buy, with side cut or without, hard or soft camber? What boots are best? These and many more questions could fill a book—and they do. Our one and only suggestion is that it may be advisable to purchase a waxless ski as your first pair. Learning to ski can be complicated enough without the frustration of trying to wax for the ever-changing snow conditions. When looking for that new pair of skis, avoid stores that just happen to have a row of cross-country skis in stock. Stores that have a special cross-country department and employees who enjoy cross-country skiing will be able to give you a better understanding of what you need and what you don't.

Cross-country boots are not noted for warmth. Two pairs of wool socks may keep the toes warm. Another help is a boot sock, which fits over the boot.

What to Take

Every skier who ventures into the wilderness should be prepared to

Cross-country skier inspecting a set of telemark turns

spend the night out. Winter storms can come with great speed and force, creating whiteouts that leave the skier with nowhere to go. Each ski pack must include the ten essentials, plus one:

1. Extra clothing—more than needed in the worst of weather.
2. Extra food—there should be some left over at the end of the trip.
3. Sunglasses—a few hours of bright sun on snow can cause a pounding headache or temporary blindness.
4. Knife—for first aid and emergency repairs.
5. First aid kit—just in case.
6. Fire starter—chemical starter to get wet wood burning.
7. Matches in a waterproof container—to start a fire.
8. Flashlight—be sure to have extra batteries with bulb.
9. Map—make sure it's the right one for the trip.
10. Compass—keep in mind the declination.
   Plus 1—Repair kit—including a spare ski tip, spare screws and binding bail (if changeable), heavy-duty tape, a few feet of braided picture wire and heavy string, and a combination wrench-pliers-screwdriver.

Other items to carry may include a small shovel, sun cream, and a large plastic tarp to use as a "picnic blanket" or for emergency shelter. All these items should fit comfortably into a day pack. Obviously, a fanny pack will not hold all the items listed above. Fanny packs are strictly for track and resort skiing where one is carrying only a sandwich and a few waxes.

Winter Camping

Most campgrounds are closed in winter by snow. However, some state parks remain open, plowing access roads and one or two campsites and offering the added attraction of heated restrooms.

When winter camping takes you out into in wilderness, camp wherever you feel safe. Avoid pitching a tent under trees heavy with snow; when least expected (day or night), "mushrooms" may fall from above and crush your tent.

Whether in the back country or on groomed tracks of a resort, carry out your garbage. (If you packed it in full, you can pack it out empty.) Burying leftovers under a few inches of snow only hides them until the spring melt. Also be careful with human waste. Hidden beneath the snow may be a stream or a summer hiking trail.

Water can be difficult to come by in winter. Most small streams are either hidden beneath the snow or flowing in grand white canyons too steep to descend. If day-skiing, carry water. On a trip lasting overnight or longer, carry a long string for lowering a bucket to an open stream as well as a stove and enough fuel to melt snow. Even in winter, the water from streams in areas where people and/or beavers and other such critters live in summer should be boiled or chemically purified.

When spending the day or several days out skiing, take care where you park your car. A sudden winter storm can make bare and dry logging roads deep in white and impossible to drive, leaving your car stranded—maybe until the spring melt. Always travel with a shovel in the car and a watchful eye on the weather.

Pets

Although in some jurisdictions the family pet is permitted to tag along on summer hikes, wintertime should be left to the two-legged family members. Skiing through knee-deep powder is lots of fun, but not for the ski-less family pet, floundering in a white morass. Pets also tend to destroy ski tracks by leaving behind deep paw prints and brown klister.

Multiple-Use

Until more areas can be designated skier-only, sharing the way with snowshoers, snowmobilers, dog sleds, and four-wheel drivers will have to be tolerated. However, multiple-use is not totally impossible. For example, in the Methow valley snowmobilers and skiers understand and respect each others' rights and needs. The snowmobilers know the difference between their machines, which destroy ski trails, and the

Don Portman reaching his stride on a groomed trail at Sun Mountain — Trail 14

Winter's delicate beauty

mechanical ski-tracking machines, which create grooves for skis. In exchange for the snowmobilers' courtesy, skiers make their tracks on the edge of a road, leaving the middle for the speeding machines.

Be Flexible

During research for this book many ranger districts and ski patrols were interviewed and one point was stressed: "Be flexible." Have an alternate, safer trip plan if weather changes to create a high avalanche potential in your favorite area. If your second choice is also unsafe, plan a walk along a beach or to the city park. Your exercise of good judgment will help ranger districts and ski areas avoid the necessity of total winter closure for *all* users in order to protect a few thoughtless ones from their own stupidity.

1 MT. BAKER TRAIL

Skill level advanced
Round trip up to 13 miles to Coleman Glacier viewpoint
Skiing time up to 2 days
Elevation gain 3700 feet
High point at least 6500 feet
Best October–November, April–mid-June
Avalanche potential low
USGS Mt. Baker

Map—page 24

From a camp near the edge of the crevasse-slashed and icefall-tumbled Coleman Glacier, set winding ski tracks through secluded bowls and across steep slopes of Heliotrope Ridge. In evening return to the doorstep of the tent and watch one of nature's best shows, a brief and brilliant winter sunset casting pinks and golds over snowy ramparts of Mt. Baker.—Or maybe crawl in the tent and peer out at a blizzard.

The route to the northwest side of Mt. Baker culminates in 3 miles of trail, but starts with 10 miles of road, some or all of which may have to be skied. Because the road is extremely popular with four-wheelers and machine skiers, cross-country skiers are advised to do this trip in fall or spring when the road is partially or totally free of snow and gas-powered travelers. A special warning about late fall: The possibility of a car's being snowed in for the winter is very real. If 6 inches of snow pile up, that is the time to leave—or be already gone.

Drive Highway 542 to Glacier and register your trip at the ranger station on the east end of town. At .6 mile past the ranger station turn right

Mt. Baker from Coleman Glacier overlook

on Glacier Creek road and follow it to the snowline or trailhead.

At 5 miles the road bumps over Coal Creek and starts serious climbing. This generally marks the beginning of spring skiing, elevation around 2000 feet. The road climbs by occasional views of Coleman Glacier and its headwall on the glacier-torn face of Mt. Baker. At a large junction at 2¾ miles take a left fork ¼ mile to the trailhead parking lot, 3700 feet.

Descend left into heavy timber to find the trail, generally discernible all winter. Skiers with skins will probably wish to use them on the steep trail. Many find it preferable to walk.

At 2 miles is Kulshan Cabin, 4700 feet, just below timberline. The cabin is open to all, but it is cold, drafty, damp, and viewless. Continue on 1 more mile to excellent campsites in scraggly trees 500 feet west of the Coleman Glacier overlook.

The best skiing lies west of the camp area, separated from it by a series of steep, slide-prone gullies. Ski up open slopes from the glacier overlook, bearing right. When the terrain levels into a broad bench at about 6500 feet, turn right and head over the rolling Heliotrope Ridge and drop down steep slopes to the bowls beyond.

Many skiers find the long open slopes leading to the summit of Mt. Baker extremely alluring. However, the attempt must not be made without climbing gear because deep crevasses lie under the smooth snow.

2 CANYON CREEK ROAD

Skill level intermediate and up
Round trip 4–10 miles
Skiing time 2–6 hours
Elevation gain up to 3000 feet
High point 5699 feet on Excelsior Peak
Best mid-March–May
Avalanche potential low
USGS Mt. Baker

Map—page 27

Throughout the winter Canyon Creek road and its many offshoots are a popular haunt of snowmobilers. However, when the spring sun starts shining and the racketeers set their snow machines aside in favor of dirt bikes, skiers will find four areas to explore out of Canyon Creek drainage.

Shoulder of Church Mtn. from the Kidney Creek road

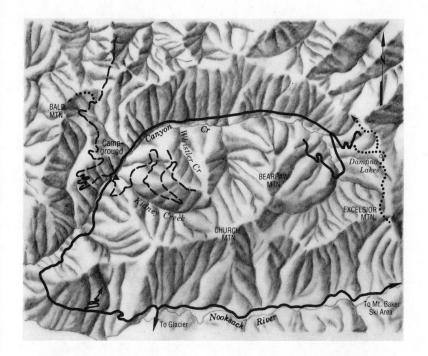

Drive Highway 542 to Glacier and 2 miles beyond. Turn left on Canyon Creek road No. 31 and go to your choice of the options below or to snowline.

Kidney Creek Road. Drive road No. 31 for 7.5 miles, then go right on road No. 3130, elevation 2150 feet, and drive to the snowline. The Kidney Creek road climbs steadily up a steep hillside, through clearcuts and forest, to an intersection at 6½ miles, 4900 feet. Here the left spur goes ½ mile north along the ridge top to views over Canyon Creek to Bald Mountain and, far on the horizon, the British Columbia Coast Range. The right fork follows the ridge top south for another mile. Advanced skiers may continue on beyond the road to open meadows below Church Mountain.

Bald Mountain Road. Drive the Canyon Creek road 8 miles from Highway 542. Cross Canyon Creek, then go left on road No. 3140, elevation 2200 feet. Follow the road 5 miles, skirting Bald Mountain, then leave the road and ski clearcuts to an open ridge top and peer over into Canada barely 1½ miles away.

Whistler Creek Road. Follow Canyon Creek road 10 miles from Highway 542, then take a right onto road No. 3160, elevation 2600 feet. Cross Canyon Creek and follow Whistler Creek 1½ miles before starting the serious climb 2½ miles to a ridge top at 4900 feet, below Bearpaw Mountain.

Excelsior Mountain Trail (recommended for advanced or mountaineer skiers). For the greatest of late, late spring skiing to spectacular views, drive road No. 31 for 15 miles from Highway 542 to the Excelsior Mountain trailhead, 4200 feet. The trail climbs through timber, gaining 300 feet in the first ¾ mile to meet the Canyon Ridge trail. Go right, passing to the east of the little Damfino Lakes, 4500 feet. Ski the next mile up through forest, then climb a gully to reach meadows at 5100 feet, 2½ miles from the road. To the south is a spectacular view of Mt. Baker and Shuksan. To the north is British Columbia, dotted with the white-topped Border Peaks and the glacier-coated Coast Range.

Telephoto view of Goat Mountain from the overlook on the Well Creek winter trail

NOOKSACK RIVER

3 WELLS CREEK

WINTER VIEWPOINT

Skill level intermediate and up
Round trip to viewpoint 6 miles
Skiing time 4 hours
Elevation gain 1100 feet
High point 2600 feet
Best mid-December–February
Avalanche potential none
USGS Mt. Baker

COUGAR DIVIDE

Skill level intermediate and up
Round trip up to 16 miles
Skiing time 2 days
Elevation gain 2400 feet
High point 4900 feet
Best April–May
Avalanche potential high in midwinter
USGS Mt. Baker

Map—page 28

In winter there is a high overlook of the Nooksack River with views from Church Mountain east to the glaciered peaks of Mt. Sefrit and Ruth Mountain crowning the Nooksack Ridge. In spring, as the snow melts back to allow vehicle access up Wells Creek road, there is the long

Cougar Divide leading to the undisputed lord of the area, Mt. Baker.

Drive Highway 542 beyond the Glacier Ranger Station 6.8 miles. A small parking area usually is plowed at the Wells Creek turnoff, elevation 1700 feet.

The winter trip starts by descending the first ½ mile to cross the Nooksack River, elevation 1500 feet, just above Nooksack Falls. (The falls trail is steep, icy, and best left for summer visits.) Beyond the river the road climbs slowly but steadily through winter-stilled forest. Just past the 2-mile marker the road forks, elevation 2000 feet. Winter skiers go left, climbing a steep road through logging clearings, noticeably messy even in winter. In 200 yards turn right and head around the edge of the clearcut at an unmarked intersection. The road climbs through young timber plantations until splitting again at 2¾ miles. The right fork wanders on another 1½ miles, heading gently downhill. The left fork climbs steeply to a flat-topped knoll with wide views. Roam the whole knoll for views from each direction. However, stay well back from the edges if not equipped with a parachute—there are cliffs with overhangs and snow cornices to the north, west, and south.

For the spring trip drive to the snowline. Be sure conditions have stabilized before setting out; open slopes below Barometer Mountain between miles 3 and 5 have a high avalanche potential after a heavy snow. At 5 miles the road leaves Wells Creek and follows Bar Creek a mile, then begins a long climb towards Cougar Divide. The road divides at the ridge top. The right fork climbs north ½ mile to an overlook of Wells Creek, 5770-foot Barometer Mountain, and Mt. Baker. The left fork heads south ½ mile along the divide. Mountaineer skiers may ski 2 more miles along the rolling crest towards the awesomely glaciered mass of Mt. Baker.

Kick-turning

NOOKSACK RIVER

4 NORTH FORK NOOKSACK RIVER ROAD

Skill level basic and up
Round trip 2–10 miles
Skiing time 2–6 hours
Elevation gain 400 feet
High point 2600 feet
Best January–mid-March
Avalanche potential low
USGS Mt. Shuksan

Map—page 31

It is unclear whether skiers are drawn to this road primarily by the nearly level terrain, the outstanding scenery, or the closure to snowmobiles. Whatever the reason, the North Fork Nooksack River road is a popular tour for novices and experts alike.

Drive Highway 542 east from Glacier 12.5 miles. Just before the highway crosses North Fork at elevation 2200 feet, the Hannegan road, start of the route, goes off left. There is no parking, so skiers must drive on .3 mile to the Sno-Park at the entrance to Silver Fir Campground and walk back.

The Hannegan road follows the North Fork Nooksack River upstream along the valley floor, open and level. Views start immediately, Mt. Shuksan gleaming in winter white, Mt. Sefrit and Ruth Mountain standing out along Nooksack Ridge.

At ½ mile cross a clearing to open forest. Several spur roads branch off in this area; stay left at all junctions. At 1½ miles the road splits. Hannegan road goes left up Ruth Creek 4 miles to the road-end at Han-

Mt. Shuksan and the North Fork Nooksack River

negan Campground, the whole way in dense forest with few views after the first mile. Avalanche hazard is high after the last mile and winter travel is not recommended. From the split the North Fork Nooksack River road goes right, skirting the north side of the valley. At 3 miles ridges close in and the valley narrows; this is a good turnaround point when the snow is unstable.

The final 2 miles climb 300 feet to the start of the Nooksack Cirque trail, not recommended for winter travel because of very high avalanche hazard.

5 ARTIST POINT

Skill level intermediate and up
Round trip 5 miles
Skiing time 3 hours
Elevation gain 1100 feet
High point 5220 feet
Best December–June
Avalanche potential low
USGS Mt. Shuksan

Map—page 33

No one who visits Artist Point on a clear day can question the name of the place, located between the vertical massif of Mt. Shuksan and the slumbering (restlessly?) dome of Mt. Baker. The scene is further embellished by hardy trees plastered with wind-driven snow like so many lonesome statues. The climb is steep, the return rapid. The trip is best done in midweek (on Monday and Tuesday, however, the road to the ski area may be unplowed) when slopes are free from the pell-mell rush of downhillers.

Drive Highway 542 east from Bellingham 55 miles to its end at the Mt. Baker Ski Area, elevation 4120 feet.

From the upper end of the parking area follow the unplowed summer road to Austin Pass. Skirt the edge of the ski area, staying off ski trails, out of the path of downhillers, and below the rope tow on Austin Pass. The serious ascent starts at the ski-area boundary; folks with climbing

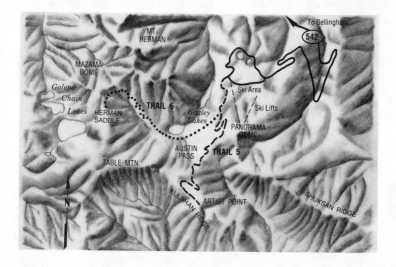

Mt. Baker from Kulshan Ridge

skins will zip by their herringboning and kick-turning comrades. At Austin Pass, 4700 feet, bear right. Skiers with climbers can take the quick route, straight up the next hill. Others will have to contour on the road to the east to gentler slopes, then climb over rolling terrain to the crest of Kulshan Ridge, 4900 feet. Be wary of a drop-off on the far side — don't let enthusiasm for the view draw you beyond the trees that mark the brink.

To the right along the ridge are imposing cliffs of Table Mountain. Turn left along Kulshan Ridge to Artist Point, 200 feet higher and ¼ mile farther. Be sure to bring a big lunch because once on Artist Point the hours disappear as in a dream amid the breathtaking beauty, which invariably includes dramatic avalanches thundering down walls of Mt. Shuksan.

6 HERMAN SADDLE

Skill level advanced
Round trip 5 miles
Skiing time 4–6 hours
Elevation gain 1060 feet
High point 5300 feet
Best December–June
Avalanche potential moderate
USGS Mt. Shuksan

Map—page 33

The Herman Saddle tour offers some of the finest downhill cross-country skiing in the western Cascades, on snow that is frequently powdery and light, down an open bowl smoother than most groomed slopes. Views of Mt. Shuksan and Mt. Baker are huge beyond Table Mountain and other foreground peaks. —And the entire tour is in plain view of tow-hill skiers on Panorama Dome.

Note: Avalanches are very common on the route, which should not be attempted after a heavy snowfall or in warming spells. In addition, the

Skiers descending the open slopes below Herman Saddle

route is easily lost in times of poor visibility. Always consult the ranger before setting out.

Drive to the Mt. Baker Ski Area parking lot, elevation 4120 feet. Begin as for Artist Point (Trail 5). At the Austin Pass rope tow drop to the old warming hut, then go left along a bench to its end. Descend to the white plain below, where the two Bagley Lakes lie hidden under a blanket of snow. See how avalanches have swept across this little basin and contemplate the foolhardiness of skiing here during periods of instability.

Cross the basin and head for Herman Saddle, the lowest and most obvious pass in the circle of peaks between Table Mountain and Mazama Dome. As the basin bends west, the ascent begins. Skiers with climbers will be glad; for those without, there commences a long series of switchbacks to gain the next 800 feet. Stay to the right side of the basin on flanks of Mt. Herman, well away from the basin headwall. Near the top, at around 5100 feet, head left (south), contouring below Mazama Dome to reach the saddle at 5300 feet. On the way up plan your descent. Decide which slopes you want to mark with graceful figure-eights (or sitzmarks) for tow-hill bunnies on Panorama Dome to admire and envy (or laugh at).

BAKER RIVER

7 PARK BUTTE

Skill level advanced
Round trip 18 miles
Skiing time 1–3 days
Elevation gain 3100 feet
High point 5000 feet
Best March–May
Avalanche potential moderate
USGS Lake Shannon and Hamilton

Map—page 37

Cross-country ski trail sign

A single day, no matter how long, is not enough for Park Butte and the adjoining flanks of Mt. Baker. Carry camping gear to insure sufficient time to tour snow-covered meadows, then climb a hill to view the Black Buttes and Twin Sisters, and watch steam rise from the volcano's crater.

Sad to say, the wide-open spaces attract snow machines like a picnic does ants. Until the Forest Service recognizes that this spectacular area is

Mt. Baker from the Park Butte ski trail

the wrong place for "racketeers," skiers will be happier if they visit late in the season or on a weekday.

Drive Highway 20 east from Sedro Woolley 14.5 miles and go left on Baker Lake road. At 12.5 miles, just after crossing Rocky Creek, turn left on Loomis–Nooksack road No. 12. In midwinter this is the starting point. In spring the road usually is open another 3.5 miles to the junction of Loomis–Nooksack road and Schreibers Meadow road No. 13, elevation 1900 feet.

Ski the right fork, road No. 13. At ½ mile a spur branches off to Dillard Point; stay left. Climb to a second spur road at 1½ miles, 2700 feet; again stay left. At 2 miles the road levels and the next 3 miles up the

Park Butte

valley are nearly flat. At 5 miles go left off road No. 13 on a well-signed, heavily traveled snowmobile track. Follow orange markers across Sulphur Creek on a wooden bridge and ½ mile to Schreibers Meadow, 3263 feet.

Turn right along Sulphur Creek to the upper end of the meadow. When the snow is stable, head up the creek between moraines. Ski up the middle of the valley to the last tree opposite the highest point of the right moraine, then turn left and traverse the relatively gentle slope to the top of the moraine. Follow the crest 100 feet, then ski through trees to a small gully which, when followed to the top at 4500 feet, gives views over the entire area.

When snow is unstable, especially after a heavy accumulation, the steep moraine walls present an avalanche hazard. In this case turn left at the upper end of Schreibers Meadow, go left and ascend the steep, narrow summer trail through forest to Park Butte.

Skier-snowmobiler "incidents" on the approach route to the meadow have stimulated the Forest Service to build a new skier trail. At this writing one section is complete, the Sulphur Creek Cutoff Trail. It starts from the Baker Lake road 300 feet south of the Shadow of Sentinels Nature Trail Sno-Park (Trail 8), climbs a steep and narrow road 2 miles to meet road No. 12 at its 2.3-mile mark, and follows this road ⅓ mile to the Rocky Creek Ski Trail. In 1982 Rocky Creek Ski Trail ends in 1½ miles at an unbridged river crossing, 2000 feet. The trail will be completed about 1984. There will *still* be racketeers in the meadows, sad to say.

8 MARTIN LAKE —MOROVITZ LOOP

Skill level basic and up
Round trip 11–30 miles
Skiing time 1–4 days
Elevation gain 1600 feet
High point 2600 feet on Boulder Ridge
Best January–mid-April
Avalanche potential none
USGS Lake Shannon and Mt. Shuksan

Map—page 39

A 4-mile approach leads to an 11-mile loop through quiet forest with sidetrip options to views, a waterfall, and a hot springs.

Drive Highway 20 east from Sedro Woolley 14.5 miles and turn left on Baker Lake–Grandy Lake road. Drive past Komo Kulshan Guard Station to the Sno-Park at the end of the plowed road at Shadow of Sentinels Nature Trail, elevation 1000 feet. (In April or in low-snow years drive 4 miles more to parking at the Boulder Creek bridge.)

Ski the highway through deep forest 4 miles. Just after crossing the Boulder Creek bridge go left, at 1040 feet, on Martin Lake road No. 1130, which climbs gently with occasional windows to Baker Lake and Mt. Shuksan between. At 1½ miles, 1275 feet, the road splits. To the left is Boulder Creek road, the first of several "must" sidetrips, a climb of 1300 feet in 4 miles to clearcuts with views of Mt. Shuksan, Park Glacier

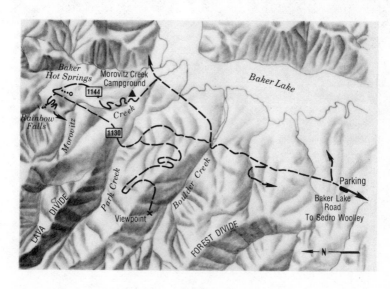

flowing from the summit of Mt. Baker, and over Baker Lake to Anderson Butte and Hagan Mountain.

The right fork, road No. 1130, descends ½ mile to cross Park Creek, then climbs 2½ miles to meet Morovitz road No. 1144 at 1600 feet. Here is the second sidetrip, to Rainbow Falls: Go left ½ mile uphill, then right on a forest trail ½ mile to the falls.

The loop goes right on road No. 1144 a short downhill mile to the next attraction, Baker Hot Springs. Due to sanitation problems, the Forest Service removed all facilities, but the trail and hot sulfur water remain. From the old parking area negotiate a short flight of steps on the right side of the road and ski the nearly level trail ¼ mile to the springs.

The loop continues 3 more miles down road No. 1144 to reach the main road at 13 miles from the Nature Trail parking lot. Ski right 2 miles to close the loop at the base of road No. 1131, then 4 miles back up the highway to finish the trip at 19 miles or—if all the sidetrips are taken—30 miles.

Baker Hot Springs

9 FINNEY CREEK ROAD

Skill level intermediate and up
Round trip 5–14 miles
Skiing time 2–8 hours
Elevation gain 500–2200 feet
High point 4400 feet
Best January–March
Avalanche potential moderate to low
USGS Oso and Finney Peak

Map—page 41

A mainline log-haul road ascends Finney Creek valley to a choice—depending on where the snowline happens to be—of six spur roads that lead to sweeping views of the North Cascades.

Drive Highway 20 to the sign marking the city limits of Concrete (don't be confused by a store–service station complex on the outskirts). Turn right on the Concrete-Sauk Valley road and follow it across the Skagit River and upstream. At 10 miles from Highway 20 turn right on Finney Creek road No. 17, a one-lane paved road with turnouts.

In a scant 3 miles, at an elevation of 790 feet, road No. 17 crosses a private logging road. If this is the snowline, ski the left fork, in 4 miles climbing to the 3000-foot level and great views.

At 5.5 miles, 770 feet, the second spur goes right on private land, in 2 miles climbing to 1800 feet and a good view of Mt. Baker.

At 8 miles, 1200 feet, find road No. 1705 on the right. This spur

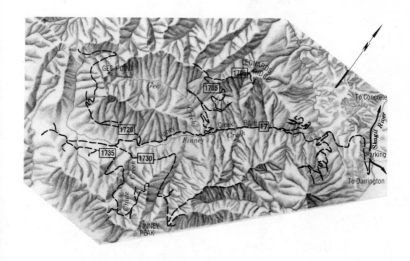

Skiing clearcut slopes above Finney Creek

switchbacks 7 miles to the 3800-foot crest of Leonards Ridge and a spectacular view of Baker, Shuksan, and mountains up and down the Skagit River.

At 10.5 miles, 1600 feet, is Gee Point road No. 1720, which winds more than 10 miles into the mountains, climbing to 4200 feet on the side of Gee Point, then dropping into the Pressentin Watershed.

At 11.5 miles the road crosses Finney Creek. At 11.8 miles, 1800 feet, it reaches road No. 1730, which traverses under the impressive face of Finney Peak, and in 7 miles, on a 4400-foot knoll, views that encompass all the North Cascades from Whitehorse Mountain to the Twin Sisters. If this is the destination, be sure to have a map to identify the endless peaks. This road crosses several avalanche chutes and should not be attempted during periods of avalanche hazard.

At 13 miles, 1900 feet, the road splits. The lower road crosses into Deer Creek drainage, and the left fork climbs 7 miles to a basin at 4200 feet on the west side of Finney Peak.

METHOW RIVER

10 CASTLE RANCH LOOP

Skill level basic and up
Loop trip 5½ miles
Skiing time 3 hours
Elevation gain none
High point 2240 feet
Best January–mid-March
Avalanche potential none
USGS Mazama

Map—page 44

Gray jay, well known
as a "Camp Robber"

Old farm buildings, open fields, dry snow, and a marked ski trail. If it weren't for towering cliffs of the Goat Wall, the scene might be somewhere along the backroads of New England. Instead, it is the Castle Ranch Loop of the Methow Valley. The trail is on private land that the owners have opened to skiers but closed to snowmobiles. Please be respectful visitors; admire the quaint old buildings, but don't explore them. If you meet the owner, be sure to thank him for his hospitality.

Castle Ranch Loop is part of a network of trails maintained by the Methow Valley Ski Touring Association. A moderate donation is asked from each skier to help cover the grooming costs. Skiers paying this donation receive a pass, good for the whole day, on any trail. Passes may be obtained at ski shops in Twisp and Winthrop or at local resorts.

Drive Highway 20 west of Winthrop 17 miles to the end of plowing at Early Winters Campground, elevation 2240 feet. Park beside the highway. A plowed county road runs north through the campground area to farms farther up the valley. The loop starts 100 feet west of this road.

For a scant ¼ mile the loop trail parallels the road in the trees, then crosses to the east side. Follow blue diamonds and ski tracks through narrow strips of forest and across fields. After ¾ mile of peaceful skiing, the trail splits. The right fork leads to the North Cascades Base Camp, reached by skiing across the sometimes frozen Methow River.

For the loop take the left fork and glide for quiet miles past farms and fences; the occasional sound of rockfall on the Goat Wall is the only reminder that this is *not* New England but the Northwest. At its north end the loop meets the county road at Castle Ranch. Continue ½ mile up the valley, circling a large fenced field at 3 miles. The return leg goes along the west edge of the valley back to the starting point at Early Winters Campground.

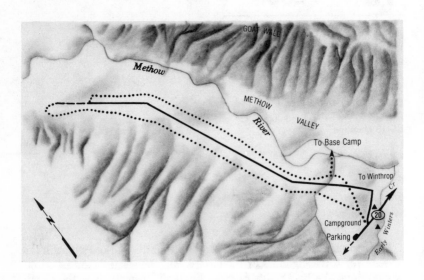

Goat Wall rises above the Methow River Valley on the Castle Ranch Loop

11 DIAMOND T RANCH –RENDEVOUS PASS

Skill level basic and up
25 miles of groomed trails
Skiing time 1 hour–4 days
Elevation gain up to 1345 feet
High point 3985 feet
Best mid-December–March
Avalanche potential none
USGS Doe Mountain and Mazama

Map—page 47

Easy or demanding, valley floor or mountain summit, one hour or several days? These are questions that must be considered before heading out over the 25 miles of groomed trails on and around Diamond T Ranch. In addition to beautiful trails, the ranch maintains a backcountry cabin equipped with stove, gas, lantern, bunks, and a picture window out on 8976-foot Mt. Gardner. Finally, there are miles of marked backcountry routes leading off the groomed trails to mountain tops overlooking the whole of northeastern Washington.

Trails in the Diamond T Ranch-Rendevous Pass are maintained by the Methow Valley Ski Touring Association. A moderate donation is

Zipping down groomed trail from Rendevous Pass

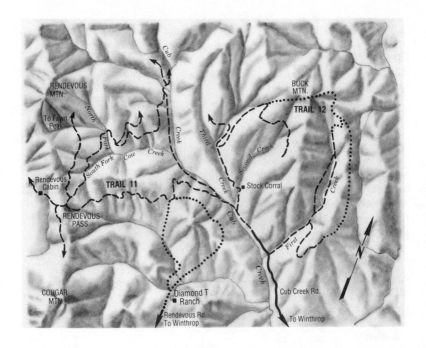

asked from each skier to help cover the grooming costs. Skiers paying this donation receive a pass, good for a whole day, on any trail. Passes may be obtained at ski shops in Twisp and Winthrop or at local resorts.

For a 1-day trip across open hills, quiet forests, and around small beaver ponds away from competing crowds, the lower trails of Diamond T Ranch are the best.

Drive Highway 20 north .1 mile from Winthrop. Turn right on West Chewack road .9 mile to Rendevous road. Go left 5.5 miles, passing Gunn Road on the left. At Diamond T Ranch entrance turn right and descend .3 mile to the parking area and the start of the trails.

For challenging mountain skiing, the 12-mile Rendevous Pass Loop is a trip for a long day or several days. The pass can be reached from Diamond T Ranch; alternatively, follow West Chewack road north 5.7 miles from the Rendevous road junction and turn left on Cub Creek road 2.5 miles to the end of plowing, elevation 2840 feet.

Ski up the road ½ mile to a Y. The right fork leads to Buck Mountain (Trail 12). Take the left fork ¼ mile down to Cub Creek and then a second left, crossing the creek 100 feet beyond. The road splits again; this is the beginning of the loop. The left fork is the shorter and steeper; skiers not wishing to descend its steep slopes, particularly when icy, should go up the left fork and return on the right.

The left fork starts climbing immediately. At 3280 feet, 2 miles from the parking area, a trail branches left towards Diamond T Ranch. Stay right and continue climbing. The two branches of the loop meet at 4 miles and join for the final ½ mile to the pass, 3985 feet.

The pass area is in trees. For views east and west ski to the left, a few hundred feet up a small knoll. For unobstructed views west to massive Mt. Gardner ski out north on the west side of the pass ½ mile towards Rendevous Cabin. Skiers wishing to stay at the cabin should contact Diamond T Ranch well in advance.

For those staying at the cabin miles of marked trails lead out from the pass area, such as a 6-mile round trip to 4614-foot Cougar Mountain, a 13-mile round trip to 6577-foot Fawn Peak, or a long descent to the Methow River Valley near Goat Creek.

The return leg of the loop has numerous windows in the forest northeast towards Buck Mountain. Watch for animal tracks, especially those of the cougar. At 9 miles, 3200 feet, take a right onto the final 2-mile leg of the loop. Skim along an old skid road paralleling Cub Creek to rejoin the up leg of the loop at 11 miles. Cross the creek and return to the starting point at 12 miles.

METHOW RIVER

12 BUCK MOUNTAIN LOOP

Skill level advanced
Loop trip 10 miles
Skiing time 7 hours
Elevation gain 1900 feet
High point 4490 feet
Best mid-December–March
Avalanche potential low
USGS Doe Mountain

Map—page 47

Buck Mountain is a perfect example of all things that have made the Methow Valley famous among cross-country skiers—open slopes for telemarking, peaceful countryside for touring, and vistas of the North Cascades and the Pasayten Mountains.

Skied from either the southwest or southeast, the two legs of the route join for a loop separated by .1-mile road walk. The southwest leg crosses open slopes and may be telemarked almost nonstop from the top to the valley floor. The southeast leg offers two different ways, both scenic, to complete the loop. The following description is for skiers who want a scenic trip up and a long fun-filled run down.

Drive Highway 20 north .1 mile from Winthrop. Turn right on West Chewack road 6.6 miles, then turn left on Cub Creek road 2.5 miles to the end of plowing, elevation 2840 feet. Walk back down the road .1 mile and turn left (north) on the primitive forest road just past First Creek. After crossing the cattle guard, the road climbs steeply up a narrow valley. At ¾ mile, 2900 feet, the road splits. To the right a scenic ridge route, longer by 2 miles, leads to the top. To the left is a shorter, but still beautiful, valley route.

Valley Route. The left fork splits again in ¼ mile. Take either left or right; they rejoin in 1 mile, forming a small loop. At the head of the valley the road ends, leaving a short, steep climb up the side of an open slope to the north to join the ridge route.

Ridge Route. The right fork climbs gently, rounding the ridge, to the road-end at 2 miles, 3200 feet. Follow blue diamonds on a traverse up to the ridge top, bypassing the first summit. Continue north, keeping a little right (east) of the ridge crest. At 3700 feet the route climbs the west side of a major knoll, then heads to the top at 5 miles, 4490 feet.

The views extend far and wide. The Chewack River valley, Paul Mountain, and Cougar Mountain are only a few of the sights. On a clear day the impressive peaks of Gardner, Midnight, and Oval are visible.

The downward route chosen will depend on the skier's ability. Begin by descending southwest, following the blue diamonds to meet a Forest Service road at 3680 feet. Ski on down, staying left at all intersections, to close the loop in 3 miles. To challenge your telemarking skills, ski this road ¼ mile from the top until a stock-loading ramp and corral are visible far below. Head down to this corral, dropping 1160 feet in almost nonstop skiing. From the bottom, follow the road down and back to your car.

Open slopes near the summit of Buck Mountain

Skier negotiating a cattle fence

METHOW RIVER

13 PIPESTONE CANYON

Skill level intermediate and up
Round trip 10 miles to head of Pipestone Canyon
Skiing time 5 hours
Elevation gain 750 feet
High point 2900 feet
Best January–mid-March
Avalanche potential low
USGS Twisp

Map—page 51

Not far above the town of Winthrop an exotically beautiful canyon lies hidden amongst the open, rolling hills. Its steep walls have been carved by wind and water into the intriguing rock formations that give the canyon its name. Located in the heart of a wildlife preserve, Pipestone Canyon can be traveled only by those with four legs or two skis.

Coming into the south end of Winthrop on Highway 20, cross the Methow River and take the first right on Main Street. In .2 mile go left on Center Street and then, in a few yards, right on Castle Avenue. Drive south 1.5 miles and turn left on Bear Creek road. Head uphill past the golf course to the pavement end in 1.8 miles. Park in a small plowed area on the right side of the road, elevation 2150 feet.

Ski Campbell Lake road up a narrow gully, climbing steadily. Cattle fences are crossed—it is essential that you restring them after passing through. At 2 miles, just after the second and last fence, the road forks. The left leads north around Bowen Mountain to Cougar Lake. Take the right fork east towards Campbell Lake. At 3½ miles the road enters a broad meadow at 2900 feet and continues over the ridge 4 miles to Beaver Creek road. Stay on the right side of the meadow to find a wind-swept road to Campbell Lake. The way descends to the south shore, the entrance to Pipestone Canyon. Continue on the road, descending the canyon ½ mile to the pipestone formation. If time allows, ski the entire 2-mile length of the canyon, losing only 480 feet. Rounded hills at the lower end offer good skiing. The quiet visitor may see deer or coyotes.

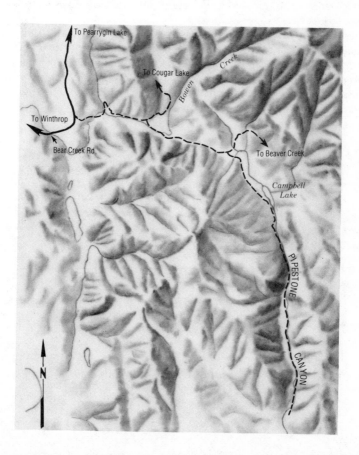

14 SUN MOUNTAIN

Skill level basic and up
Nearly 20 miles of trails
Skiing time 3 hours–all day
Elevation gain 1387 feet
High point 3987 feet
Best January–mid-March
Avalanche potential low
USGS Buttermilk Butte

Map—page 52

Sun Mountain Lodge is perched 1000 feet above the Methow Valley in the center of a network of groomed and/or marked cross-country trails that lead to scenic overlooks, mountain passes, and lakes. Whether novice or veteran, any skier will appreciate the way miles skim by on prepared tracks.

Drive Highway 20 north from Twisp 5.3 miles. Turn left on Twin Lake road 1.8 miles and go left on Patterson Lake road 5.6 miles to Sun Mountain Lodge. Stop by the ski shop for a map and further information about trails. Parking at the lodge itself is for guests, but just .5 mile below the lodge is a public parking area, elevation 2700 feet; a small donation is asked to help maintain the trail system.

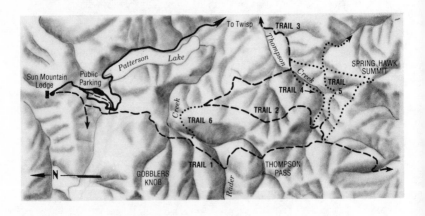

Trail 1   Thompson Ridge road
Trail 2   Meadow Lark Trail
Trail 3   Upper Pine Forest Trail
Trail 4   Woody Trail
Trail 5   Diving Hawk Trail
Trail 6   Cutoff Trail

Skiing the prepared tracks at Sun Mountain resort

Enjoyable day trips can be made from the lodge or public parking lot. Follow the Ridge Route to Hough Homestead Shelter or the Beaver Pond Trail to the beaver pond; telemarkers like to climb to the top of Herringbone Hill to swish down.

The Soaring Hawk Loop is a combination of groomed trails and an exciting off-track route for intermediate skiers. From the public parking lot cross the main road to the snow-covered Thompson Ridge road. Stay with the groomed road 4 miles to a major intersection, 3480 feet, with the Diving Hawk ski trail. Leave the groomed trail and climb the ridge between the two roads. Pass to the left of the first knob and go across a shallow saddle. Make the final ascent to the top of Soaring Hawk at 5 miles, 3987 feet.

From this high perch the view extends to hundreds of Cascade peaks, over Elbow Coulee, and across the Methow Valley. Return the way you came or do a loop, testing telemarking skills by descending the open, forested slopes of Soaring Hawk's northeast side. Ski across the Diving Hawk Trail to meet Upper Pine Forest Trail; close the loop by following this trail to the Cut-Off Trail, which leads to the Thompson Ridge road and back to Sun Mountain Lodge or the parking lot.

15 METHOW VALLEY TRAIL (M.V.T.)

Skill level basic and up
One way 19 miles
Skiing time 5 hours–2 days
Maximum elevation gain 1000 feet
High point 2600 feet
Best January–mid-March
Avalanche potential low
USGS Twisp

Map—page 55

The Methow Valley Trail isn't what the name suggests. It's not really a valley trail at all, except that it gives grand views the length and width of the valley as it climbs to ridge tops, winds around frozen lakes, and passes overlooks.

The trail may be skied as a whole or in sections. Here the trail is described in three parts, from south to north.

Twisp to Elbow Coulee. This 8-mile section is the most scenic, traversing wild, open country with broad vistas and miles of hills to explore. A 1000-foot ascent and a steep 200-foot descent at the end make it best

Methow Valley Trail near Twisp

suited for skiers of intermediate level and up. The trail is marked by blue-painted stakes which often are difficult to spot; be sure to carry a contour map.

Drive Highway 20 north from Twisp town center, cross the Twisp River at the edge of town, and take the first left. Follow this street .3 mile and take the first left for .2 mile. The road makes a sharp bend at elevation 1610 feet; find a parking place well off the street.

Climb north to an open terrace on an old jeep road, cross the terrace, and follow a narrow gully left. Pass to the left of snow-covered Peters Puddles and turn left up another long, open hill. At the top follow a spur road west down to Dead Horse Lake, 2300 feet, at 4 miles. The spur leads to a forest road, the route for the next 3 miles. If time allows, at the 6½-mile point make a ½-mile sidetrip to Aspen Lake. At 7 miles the road ends. The final mile drops to Elbow Coulee road, 2400 feet.

Elbow Coulee to Patterson Lake. This is the least-demanding section, 4 miles long, gaining only 100 feet, following a groomed trail through open timber and around Patterson Lake.

Easiest access is from the north end at Patterson Lake Resort, 1 mile below Sun Mountain Lodge (Trail 14).

This section is groomed by the Methow Valley Ski Touring Association. Skiers are asked to give a moderate donation to help cover costs. In return for the donation, skiers receive a pass, good for a whole day, on any trail. Passes may be obtained at ski shops in Twisp and Winthrop or at local resorts.

Patterson Lake to Winthrop (Virginian Motel). This 6-mile section, all in open country, descends 740 feet to the valley floor. It is best for intermediate level and up.

Park at Patterson Lake Resort and walk .1 mile along the road to the end of the lake, elevation 2500 feet. Pass through a small gate and ski down a narrow gully, following the markers. The trail drops 500 feet in the first mile, then turns right around the base of Patterson Mountain. Cross Twin Lakes road at 3 miles. The final stretch, nearly level, is out in the open with views of glistening white hills to the east. The trail ends at Highway 20, elevation 1740 feet, 1¼ miles south of Winthrop and ⅓ mile south of the Virginian Motel.

The Methow Valley Trail, designed and maintained by local citizens and businesses, crosses both public and private land; please respect property rights. It is hoped ultimately to connect the trail to the Diamond T system (Trail 11) and then drop down Mazama to end at Castle Ranch (Trail 10).

METHOW RIVER

16 LOUP-LOUP

Skill level basic and up
Loop trip 4 miles
Skiing time 3 hours
Elevation gain 100 feet
High point 4100 feet
Best December–March
Avalanche potential none
USGS Loup-Loup

Map—page 58

Applying liquid glider to no-wax skis

What better place to ski a loop than on the Loup-Loup? Actually the name may have nothing to do with circles, but rather stems from the French word for wolf (*loup*); whether or not this particular *loup* ran in circles through the open forest is a fact that has been lost in history.

Loup-Loup Trail, maintained by the Methow Valley Ski Touring Association and the Ide-A-Wile Inn, is regularly groomed and signed with blue diamonds. Though terrain is rolling, the way maintains a near-constant elevation. Numerous sidetrips to ridge tops or along roads can extend the tour to a long day or several long days.

Drive Highway 20 to Loup-Loup Pass, elevation 4000 feet, located 10.5 miles east of the junction of Highways 20 and 153 and 18 miles west of Okanogan. Park at the summit in the plowed space on the south side of the highway.

Ski the South Summit road, a combination skier-snowmobile route. In a scant ¼ mile an overlook gives views down the length of Fraser Creek to magnificent peaks of the North Cascades. In another long ½ mile is an intersection where snow machines are directed to the right;

skiers turn left and climb a short, steep hill to the start of the loop. To avoid chaos with other skiers, do the loop in a clockwise direction.

At the top of the hill bear left. (The trail to the right will be the return leg.) Cruise through open timber where animal tracks abound; watch for rabbit tracks followed by coyote tracks. Unless directed otherwise, at junctions with all the numerous sideroads stay right for the basic loop. (Supplied with an up-to-date Forest Service map or Green Trails map, skiers can explore these untracked sideroads on great loops lasting several days.) The Loup-Loup trail meanders through quiet forest with many attractive spots for a picnic. The loop closes at 3¼ miles and the final ¾ mile follows the road back to the summit parking area.

Methow Valley from the Loup-Loup Trail

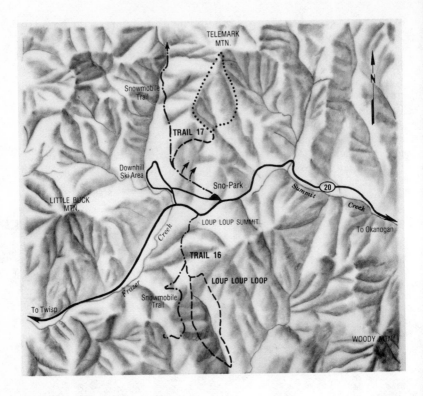

17 TELEMARK MOUNTAIN

Skill level advanced
Round trip to summit 6 miles
Skiing time 4 hours
Elevation gain 1512 feet
High point 5532 feet
Best January–March
Avalanche potential moderate
USGS Loup-Loup

Map—page 58

A steep climb without an established trail leads to far views. Telemark Mountain has good snow the whole season but is especially noted for fine spring skiing. The steep slopes have an 800-foot vertical drop, perfect for sweeping runs. Energetic skiers may repeat the trip several times in an afternoon.

Drive Highway 20 east from Winthrop toward Okanogan. At .3 mile past Loup-Loup Summit turn north on the access to the downhill ski area, .1 mile to a Sno-Park, elevation 4020 feet.

Before starting out take some time to get a feel for the terrain because beyond the road-end the navigation through the trees is strictly seat-of-the-pants. To the north the large hill with open slopes and a few trees crowning the summit is Telemark Mountain. The route follows the west ridge to the top.

Head north from the Sno-Park, as do most of the machine tracks. The machines themselves are rarely on hand except weekends, when they arrive in large packs. However, Methow Valley snowmobilers are some of the most polite in the country; stay to the side of the road and your space will be respected.

Keep count of not-so-obvious spur roads to the right. Take the third; if you come to a major forest road, you've gone too far—turn around and recount. Follow this spur about 1 mile, then ascend to the ridge and ski northeast along the crest. Just before the main mass of the mountain, dip off the crest briefly to get around a small rock haystack. The summit, 5532 feet, provides an overlook of a good portion of the Okanogan country, miles and miles over rolling hills almost to the Columbia River.

In good weather and stable snow, descend open slopes on the south to a small basin, then contour west (right) to rejoin your uphill tracks. During times of high avalanche hazard go down the way you came up—no hardship because it also is good skiing.

Tracks of a snowshoe hare

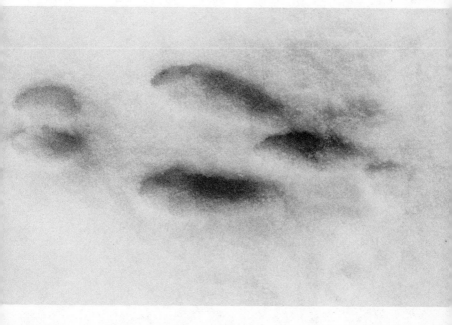

18 GREEN MOUNTAIN

Skill level mountaineer
Round trip from road-end 8 miles
Skiing time 6 hours
Elevation gain 3000 feet
High point 6530 feet
Best December or May
Avalanche potential moderate
USGS Downey Mountain

Map—page 61

Because of a long road approach and high avalanche potential throughout the winter, Green Mountain is best reserved for early- or late-season tours. As soon as the emerald meadows are covered by their

Glacier Peak from the Green Mountain ski trail

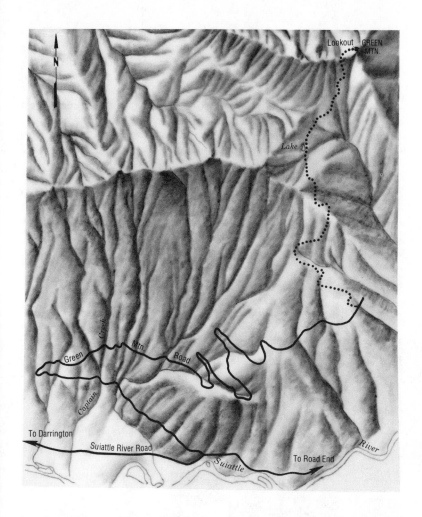

first foot of snow, skiing is excellent on the steep, open slopes amid views of the North Cascades from Mt. Baker all the way to a glimpse of Mt. Rainier. In spring the timing is trickier. A party must wait until the road melts open and the snowpack stabilizes to solid corn, but not so long that the snow is more water than snow — or has gone into summer hibernation. The timing for views, however, is not difficult to figure. It just takes good weather.

Drive north from Darrington or south from Rockport to Suiattle River road No. 26 and follow it 19 miles to Green Mountain road No. 2680, elevation 1300 feet. Follow the road for 5 miles to its end at 3500 feet or until blocked by snow or slides.

Green Mountain Trail starts on a forested hillside 300 feet before the road-end. Ski or hike the steep trail the first mile through dense timber to treeline at the edge of open meadows, 4200 feet. (If the trail is lost in timber, ski steeply up from the parking lot with a slight lean to the left.)

At treeline skirt left around the edge of the meadows, keeping in the shelter of the trees and avoiding several obvious avalanche tracks. At the end of the meadows turn uphill and climb 200 feet to a slanting bench in the protection of trees.

Traverse to the right, ascending across the bench, using as much forest cover as possible. Once on the east side of the slope, ski to the ridge top. Follow the crest up another 500 feet and then traverse right to a tree-dotted shelf leading to a small snow-covered lake in a deep bowl, 5220 feet.

Before reaching the lake choose your route to the lookout on the 6530-foot summit of Green Mountain. Left from the lake pick up a steep shoulder and follow it up. Or, when the snow is stable, go right and ski up the middle of the open south slope to the first saddle west of the lookout and join the ridge route for the final ascent. Unwrap the sandwiches and gaze at Mt. Buckindy (just to the north), Dome Peak, Baker, and Shuksan. To the south stand Glacier Peak, White Chuck, Pugh, and Sloan.

Avalanche lilies

19 NORTH MOUNTAIN

Skill level intermediate and up
Round trip 2-28 miles
Skiing time 2 hours-2 days
Elevation gain up to 3000 feet
High point 4000 feet
Best January-April
Avalanche potential low
USGS Darrington, Fortson, and Finney Peak

Map—page 63

The North Lookout road offers views from lazy, damp valley bottoms to a crisp polar display of Whitehorse, Higgins, Pugh, Glacier Peak, White Chuck, Mt. Baker, and even the Pickets. The numerous spurs provide destinations suitable for whatever amount of time is available and from wherever the snowline may be. An overnight snowfall may divert a party from a planned ridge cruise to valley wanderings.

Drive Highway 530 to Darrington. Continue on the highway north .7 mile past Darrington Ranger Station and turn left on paved road No. 28. At 2.5 miles is a major intersection, elevation 1000 feet, the usual winter starting point for skiers.

The right fork, road No. 2810, goes to Texas Pond and North Lookout, the recommended destination when the machine-sitting crowd is not out in force. Ski 3½ miles, gaining 1000 feet, then take a right and switchback another 6½ miles up open slopes to a tremendous viewpoint at the 3956-foot lookout. In winter this is an overnight destination; in March and April, when the road can be driven farther, it's an easy day.

For shorter trips or on days when the machines are marauding take the lower left fork at the 1000-foot intersection. The road remains at a near-

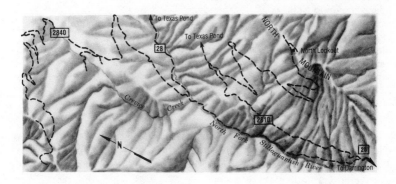

North Mountain Lookout

constant elevation 4 miles to the crossing of the North Fork Stilla-guamish River. In ¼ mile more the road splits. When the snow level is low, the right fork may be followed beside the river for 5 miles to Texas Pond, 1400 feet. The left fork, road No. 2840, winds 12 miles up to an end on a 4000-foot ridge top. Clearcuts along the way provide a succession of vistas; views from the top are superb.

DARRINGTON

20 SEGELSEN CREEK ROAD

Skill level intermediate and up
Round trip up to 24 miles
Skiing time 2 hours–2 days
Elevation gain up to 3000 feet
High point 3431 feet at Deer Creek Pass
Best January–April
Avalanche potential low
USGS Fortson

Map—page 65

A week could be spent skiing here without covering the whole area, which extends from near-rainforest on the valley floor to open ridges 3000 feet above with views out to a formidable lineup of glaciered and snow-clad Cascade giants.

As with all the local roads, Segelsen Creek has an extremely variable snowline. Depending on whims of the weather, skiers from January through March may start at the absolute bottom—or 5 miles up. Only the spring skier can reasonably hope to drive more than the first few miles. However, the skiing is fun and the views are good no matter where the capricious snowline is.

Drive Highway 530 east from Arlington 24 miles to the small community of Whitehorse. Just opposite the Whitehorse Mercantile (gas station and store) turn left on Swede Heaven road 1.7 miles, crossing the railroad tracks and bridge and passing fields. Go right on Segelsen Creek road No. 18. Trip mileages in the following description start from this intersection, elevation 420 feet.

The way climbs through a tunnel of moss-covered trees. At 2 miles a

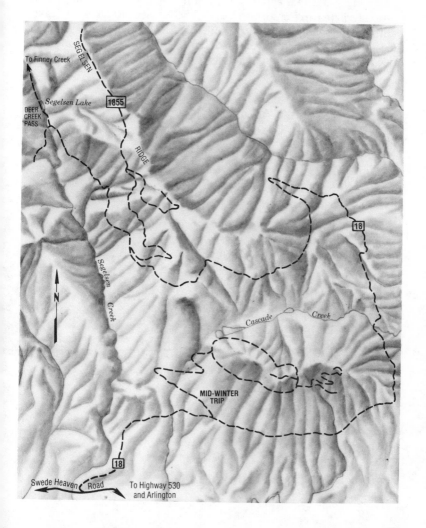

spur road heads sharply back left. When the snow level is low, follow this steeply climbing road as far as energy and ambition will take you. Be sure to reach at least one clearcut for views over fields and farms in the valley below and to glacier-carved Whitehorse Mountain filling the horizon beyond. Armed with an up-to-date Green Trails or Forest Service map, ski to the top of bald knolls (the highest is 2685 feet) or design loops on the intertwining spur roads.

The supreme scenery lies higher than the spur road will take you. If possible, therefore, continue on road No. 18. Good views start at about 9 miles from Swede Heaven road and continue to Segelsen Creek road's high point, Deer Creek Pass, 3431 feet, at 12 miles. Be treated to views of innumerable peaks, some of them recognizable summer favorites like Glacier Peak, White Chuck, Whitehorse, Bedal, and Pugh, plus a host of less famous peaks that appear quite distinguished in their winter whites.

An alternate trip for spring skiers is the Segelsen Ridge road. Take a right fork off road No. 18 at 9½ miles, 3250 feet, and follow road No. 1855 as it climbs steeply 1½ miles to the 4300-foot ridge. Skim along the ridge top for 2 miles of limitless views.

Whitehorse Mountain from the Segelsen Creek road

21 PILCHUCK MOUNTAIN ROAD

Skill level intermediate and up
Round trip 14 miles
Skiing time 6 hours-2 days
Elevation gain 2120 feet
High point 3120 feet
Best January-February
Avalanche potential low
USGS Granite Falls

Map—page 67

Decorated sign along the Pilchuck Mountain road

Pilchuck Mountain once was the scene of bustling winter activity as cars drove bumper to bumper up a winding road 7 miles to ski one of Washington's most challenging downhill runs. Lodge skiers, avoiding the embarrassments of cliff skiing, were once treated to an excellent view across Robe Valley to 6854-foot Three Fingers. Today the lifts and crowds have gone, beaten by poor weather and too many cliffs for beginners. However, the views and an excellent skiing road remain—all the better because nowadays the road after the first 1½ miles is reserved

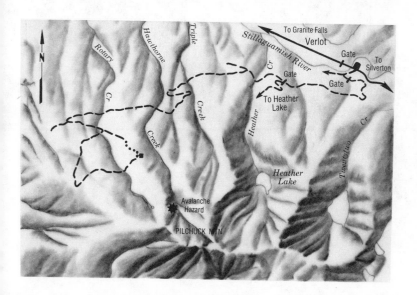

Three Fingers Mountain from the old Pilchuck Mountain downhill ski area

in winter for nonmotorized use. The parking area at the top makes a comfortable and scenic campsite and the once-groomed slope below the old lodge is ideal for a little downhill-telemark practice.

Drive Mountain Loop Highway, 1 mile east of Verlot Ranger Station. Immediately after crossing the South Fork Stillaguamish River, turn right on Pilchuck road, in midwinter often gated at this point. Early- and late-season skiers may be able to drive another 1.5 miles to a second gate, closed all winter, where all motorized vehicles must stop. Park in the Heather Lake Trail parking area, elevation 1400 feet.

Intriguing though the lake trail may be, after the first ½ mile it becomes steep and narrow in deep forest, unsuitable for skiing.

The Pilchuck road climbs steadily, passing several spurs that offer sidetrips. The two most interesting are just below the 2- and 5-mile markers. Both roads wind through clearcuts with long views north and west. After 5 miles the road levels somewhat as it starts a long switchback that ends 2 scenic miles later at the old ski area.

Skiers wishing to climb higher will find easy access across the old ski slope above the lodge. An old service road begins a short way up the slope on the right side, winds through the trees, and reemerges just below the summit of the first hill. Beyond this point the route is difficult, ascending steep slopes and a short cliff to the top of the old ski area. Ski ascents of 5324-foot Pilchuck should be confined to late spring; avalanche potential on the upper mountain is extreme.

On the return, advanced skiers may shortcut by descending the open slope below the lodge. Near the bottom left a logging spur can be picked up that rejoins the main road just above the 5-mile marker.

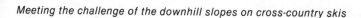

Meeting the challenge of the downhill slopes on cross-country skis

22 DEER CREEK ROAD

Skill level intermediate and up
Round trip to road-end 8½ miles
Skiing time 6 hours
Elevation gain 1500 feet
High point 3100 feet
Best January–March
Avalanche potential low
USGS Silverton

Map—page 70

The particular appeal of Deer Creek is that it is one of two areas along the South Fork Stillaguamish River (the other being Mt. Pilchuck) reserved for nonmotorized sports. Once past the throngs of exuberant snow-players, skiers will find peaceful forest, snow-shrouded clearcuts, and awesome views of rough peaks.

Drive Mountain Loop Highway east from Verlot Ranger Station 12.1

Deer Creek

miles to the end of plowing at Deer Creek road No. 4052. Turn left and park in the large snow-play lot, elevation 1600 feet.

Taking care to dodge out-of-control sledders, follow Deer Creek road steeply up dense second-growth to a small knob. In the first ½ mile two spurs branch off; stay left at both. At 1 mile, 2000 feet, the Double Eagle road (Trail 23) heads east. Continue left on Deer Creek road, climbing steadily northwest, deeper into the long valley towards Bald Mountain at its head, impressive in its cloak of snow.

The best views are in a vast clearcut at 2½ miles, soon after the first crossing of Deer Creek; look down the valley to Hall Peak, Big Four, and jagged summits of the Monte Cristo group. In a scant ½ mile more the road abruptly turns north, away from Bald Mountain, and ascends a final 1¼ miles to its end in a clearcut just beyond the second crossing of Deer Creek. The return is a long, fun glide.

Near the road-end two trails take off. The upper one, best suited to snowshoers, climbs ½ mile through forest to Deer Creek Pass. The lower one, starting just past Deer Creek, leads a scant ½ mile to Kelcema Lake; it is negotiable by experienced skiers, brave intermediates, and beginners proficient in using tree trunks and branches to slow their descent. The route is not well marked but can be followed to the lake by keeping about 500 feet right of the creek the whole way. On the east shore are several sheltered campsites.

Double Eagle road

23 DOUBLE EAGLE ROAD

Skill level advanced
Round trip 8 miles
Skiing time 5 hours
Elevation gain 1500 feet
High point 3100 feet
Best January–March
Avalanche potential low
USGS Silverton

Map—page 70

The Deer Creek "muscle-powered sports preserve" is a place for the human spirit to run free, unshackled by machinery. Families with children need only sleds and innertubes to enjoy a winter wonderland more fun than Disneyland. Skiers can enjoy watching the rocketing and screaming kids—and then proceed onward to quiet, peace, and dramatic views of peaks from Monte Cristo to Pilchuck.

Drive to the Deer Creek snow-play parking lot (Trail 22), elevation 1600 feet. Ski Deer Creek road 1 mile and turn right on gated Double Eagle road No. 4054, which climbs rapidly at first, then settles into a lesser, but steady, ascent. After 1 mile of forest, vistas begin. Look out across the Stillaguamish valley to Big Four Mountain, its great north face ribboned by avalanche chutes, and to next-door Sperry Peak, and look easterly to peaks of the Monte Cristo group. Across Coal Creek valley the aftermath of massive clearcutting is revealed in miles of open slopes leading to Coal and Independence lakes.

The Double Eagle road is wide enough at the start for two-way traffic. Higher, the brush closes in, just permitting skiers to sneak through. At 3¾ miles the road drops a bit, then abruptly quits, at a perfect spot to have lunch and soak in the scenery from Monte Cristo to Pilchuck.

The return tends to be rapid and in icy conditions a little tricky. Watch for rabbits, squirrels, and their tracks. But don't be distracted from the rocky wall which borders the road in several sections; on warm days a stone or two may be shed.

SOUTH FORK STILLAGUAMISH RIVER

24 BIG FOUR PICNIC AREA

MOUNTAIN LOOP HIGHWAY

Skill level basic and up
Round trip to picnic area 5 miles
Skiing time 3 hours
Elevation gain 180 feet
High point 1780 feet
Best January–mid-March
Avalanche potential none
USGS Silverton

COAL CREEK LOOP

Skill level intermediate and up
Loop trip 6 miles
Skiing time 4 hours
Elevation gain 400 feet
High point 2000 feet
Best January–mid-March
Avalanche potential low
USGS Silverton

Map—page 70

The Mountain Loop Highway makes a splendid ski trail. The valley bottom is gently rolling; the lush forest, moss-hung trees, snowbound Stillaguamish River, and steep-walled mountains are superbly scenic. A

There is excellent skiing in the small meadows, picnic areas, and campgrounds along the Mountain Loop Highway

perfect tour? Not quite. Due to the relatively low elevation, the highway provides an easy entry to the wonders of winter and on a fine Sunday half the snow-players in the state pour into the valley. Four-wheelers come in trucks and jeeps to "see how far they can get." Innocent family sedans trustingly follow the ruts, high-center, and get stuck, can't turn around, and have to be pulled out by four-wheelers. Snow machines razz through the tangle, dog sleds mush by, snowshoers web, hikers slog. It's a mindtwister as hard as Rubik's Cube to unravel, but not so hot for skiing. For *that* the best time is the middle of the week—and/or immediately after a heavy snowfall that scares out even the jeep heroes. Ah, peace! Ah, the joy of making a single, quiet track through virgin snows in the virgin forest!

In addition to the straight-shot ski run up the highway to Big Four Picnic Area, a traffic-escaping loop can be made via Coal Lake road. The trip also can be extended up the highway to other scenic objectives.

Drive to the Deer Creek snow-play parking lot (Trail 22), elevation 1600 feet.

Head east. In ½ mile cross Coal Creek and pass road No. 4057, the return leg of the loop trip described below. At 2½ miles is Big Four Picnic Area, in a meadow where a resort hotel was located until 1949 when it burned to the ground. The mountain is still there, 6135-foot Big Four, tall and cold, and when the sun touches it, roaring with avalanches.

A popular winter walk is the 1-mile trail (not skiable) to—or near— the ice caves. Stay well within the trees to be safe from the avalanches that pile up the snows in which the ice caves are formed by creeks and winds.

To return via the loop, continue on the highway a bit beyond the picnic area and turn left on Coal Lake road No. 4060. In ½ mile pass a fork to the right, take the first fork to the left, road No. 4062. Ski down clearcuts, then over the valley bottom, 2 miles to the road-end. Follow the marked trail through forest to road No. 4057. Turn left ¼ mile to return to the highway just above Coal Creek.

When not chopped up by machines, the Mountain Loop Highway makes a good ski trail beyond Big Four to Barlow Pass, 8 miles, except for a short stretch above Perry Creek, which poses an avalanche hazard in unstable conditions.

Another scenic tour is Sunrise Mine road. At 5 miles turn off the highway on road No. 4065, which in 2 miles enters a beautiful cirque. Avalanche potential is high along the mine road and in the cirque.

Coal Lake road

25 COAL LAKE

Skill level intermediate and up
Round trip up to 14½ miles
Skiing time 5 hours–2 days
Elevation gain 2160 feet
High point 3760 feet
Best January–April
Avalanche potential moderate
USGS Silverton

Map—page 70

The road to Coal Lake does two great things: (1) It escapes the main traffic flow of the Mountain Loop Highway and (2) leads to fantastic views of peaks from Mt. Pilchuck to Big Four Mountain and Sperry Peak and much more. As everywhere throughout the Stillaguamish valley, the roar of snow machines echoes, and lonesomeness is not to be expected. A Nordic skier with a little adventure in the heart, however, can find a day or more of peace at Coal Lake.

Drive to the Deer Creek snow-play parking lot (Trail 22), elevation 1600 feet.

Ski the Mountain Loop Highway (Trail 24) 2½ miles. A short bit beyond the turnoff to Big Four Picnic Area go left at a sign pointing to Coal Lake road No. 4060.

The road climbs gradually in forest that soon thins to open vistas on the Stillaguamish valley and surrounding peaks. The great north wall of

Big Four dominates, but other mountains have their say.

Avalanche hazard is low until about ¾ mile from the lake. Just before the road enters into heavy timber a short, 200-foot open stretch of slopes must be watched. Spot the lake on the right side of the road; there are some very nice campsites.

For further explorations continue on an unmarked path to Pass Lake or Independence Lake.

The run home is gentle but sometimes rapid. It has a few tight corners, so don't get distracted by the view.

Del Campo Peak from the Coal Lake road

26 MILLER RIVER

Skill level basic and up
Round trip 4–15 miles
Skiing time 3 hours–2 days
Elevation gain up to 2100 feet
High point 3058 feet at Lake Dorothy
Best January–March
Avalanche potential low
USGS Grotto, Skykomish, and Snoqualmie Lake

Map—page 77

Moss-draped trees, rivers, waterfalls, and spots for viewing mountain goats in their winter quarters on valley cliffs. The route begins on a logging road through rainforest-like vegetation with looks up to 5591-foot Cascade Mountain. Advanced skiers may continue on a 1½-mile trail into the Alpine Lakes Wilderness to Lake Dorothy, with views of snow-covered Big Snow Mountain.

Drive Highway 2 east to the Miller River road 2.7 miles west of Skykomish, and at the Money Creek Campground sign turn right on the old Cascade Highway. At 1 mile turn right on Miller River road. In about 100 feet pass Money Creek road on the right and continue straight to the end of the plowed road at the Miller River Campground, elevation 1040 feet.

From the intersection go right and glide along beside Miller River in dense timber 1½ miles. When the West Fork road branches off right, keep left and cross the West Fork Miller River. At ⅛ mile beyond the bridge is the first of the two goat-viewing spots; from a turnout on the left side of the road gaze across the valley, watching the cliffs for little snowpatches that walk. In times of high avalanche potential, make this the turnaround, avoiding a dangerous chute 1 mile ahead.

The second goat-viewing spot is the East Fork Miller River bridge at 3 miles. In ½ mile more, at 1700 feet, is another bridge of note—of note because it isn't there, washed out in a lovely flood, and if wilderness-

Lunch break on Camp Robber Creek bridge along the trail to Lake Dorothy

lovers have a say, never to be replaced. However, skis may have to come off to cross the bouldery gap.

The road ends in 2½ miles more, 6 miles from Miller River Campground, at the Lake Dorothy trailhead, 2100 feet. The trail takes off from the far right end of the (former) parking area and is so wide that it is fairly easy to follow even when deep in snow.

At 1 mile, 2480 feet, the trail crosses Camp Robber Creek—just as it joins Miller River—on a wide bridge overlooking a pretty series of cascades. From here head straight up into a basin, contour its headwall, and climb steadily northwest to the lake outlet, 3058 feet.

The lakeshore trail offers 2 more miles of easy touring. Camping is good all along the east shore.

27 FOSS RIVER

Skill level basic and up
Round trip 2-20 miles
Skiing time 1 hour-4 days
Elevation gain 100-2960 feet
High point 4800 feet
Best December-May
Avalanche potential low-moderate
USGS Skykomish, Big Snow Mountain, and Mt. Daniel

Map—page 80

From the first snowfall of late autumn to those rocky last runs of early summer, and in all the months in-between, there are Foss River trails to engage skiers at any level. Each trail has a special scenic character, whether of serene valley floor or icy-craggy Alpine Lakes Wilderness.

Drive Highway 2 east 1.8 miles from Skykomish and turn right on Foss River road No. 68. At 1.2 miles turn right again. At 2.5 miles pass under a railroad trestle to the winter parking area, elevation 1280 feet.

Tonga Ridge. In early and late season the best skiing is on Tonga Ridge, which offers numerous viewpoints of Mt. Baring, Glacier Peak,

Foss River

and the ramparts leading to Mt. Daniel. The route is not recommended in midwinter due to (1) snowmobilers and (2) avalanches which somehow fail to eliminate (1). Though basic skiers may be able to carry skis up and down the steep forest trail, the trip is not recommended for those below the intermediate level.

From the winter parking area continue up Foss River road to 3.6 miles from Highway 2 and turn left on Tonga Ridge road No. 6830. At 13.6 miles, 3880 feet, the road's highest point, find a spur on the right, signed "Tonga Ridge." Ski (or drive, as the case may be) 1½ miles up the steep spur to its end and the trailhead, 4400 feet.

The trail begins by abruptly gaining 200 feet up the edge of a clearcut, then climbs a mile of forest to meadows of the Alpine Lakes Wilderness. The upsy-downsy way contours another 2 miles around Sawyer Mountain to Sawyer Pass, 4800 feet.

Foss River Road. Except for the first mile, the Foss River road is reserved for nonmotorized sports and most snowmobilers abide by the rule. The Forest Service additionally has marked three ski trails into the Alpine Lakes Wilderness. This road therefore can be heartily recommended for an afternoon or overnight tour during the loudest months of winter.

From the 1280-foot parking area ski the long, flattish mile to the Tonga Ridge road, passing a rock wall that may display a fantasy of icicles. At the junction go straight ahead.

At 2 miles pass the East Fork Foss River trail; this is a very nice sidetrip for intermediate skiers, 5 miles up a U-shaped valley. Stop when the trail turns west, crossing the east fork to start its 3-mile climb up to Necklace Valley. This final section has a high avalanche potential throughout the winter.

At 2½ miles on Foss River road a spur leads to West Fork Foss River trail, another possible sidetrip, 3 miles but quite difficult and avalanche prone before any view is possible.

The Foss River road crosses the West Fork of the Foss River bridge at 2¾ miles then starts its long climb up steep open slopes to Maloney Ridge. The bridge is a good turnaround point when conditions are unstable.

At 6½ miles keep right at a major junction, and continue to the radio tower at 9 miles, 3364 feet. The views extend up and down the Skykomish River to Mt. Index, Mt. Baring, and Glacier Peak. To see Mt. Daniel and Mt. Hinman follow the road to Sobieski Mountain at 12 miles, 4400 feet.

Mt. Baring, Merchant and Gunn Peaks from Tonga Ridge

28 BECKLER PEAK ROAD

Skill level intermediate and up
Round trip 3–14 miles
Skiing time 2 hours–2 days
Elevation gain up to 2900 feet
High point 4200 feet
Best March–April
Avalanche potential low
USGS Skykomish and Grotto

Map—page 82

Views and more views. Ski high above the Beckler River to overlooks down the South Fork Skykomish River and up Money Creek. Continuing up the road, gaze southward over the Foss River to a multitude of peaks in the Alpine Lakes Wilderness. Though called the Beckler Peak road, loggers have extended it on a long, nearly level traverse east to Alpine Baldy, where it ends at about 4200 feet. At 1½, 2, and 3 miles are excellent views and rewarding turnarounds.

The Beckler Peak road is a designated snowmobile trail, but the relatively short length and lack of midwinter parking generally leave it free from machine hassle. Skiers have the same parking problems as snowmobilers. The only winter space currently available is along the side of Highway 2, where parking is allowed unless a snowplow wishes to clear the area, a frequent occurrence. The best idea is to wait until spring, when the low elevations melt out, leaving ample parking and shorter access to the high viewpoints.

Drive Highway 2 east of Skykomish 3.5 miles and turn left (north) on Beckler Peak road No. 66. Drive 2 miles, crossing under powerlines,

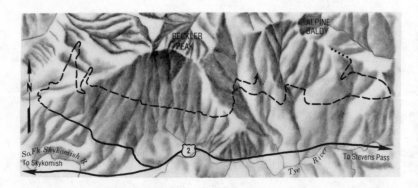

Skykomish River Valley from Beckler Peak road

then northeast around the base of the peak to the beginning of this trip, elevation 1240 feet.

Walk or drive to the snowline, following the switchbacking road as it climbs briskly through a jungle-like tangle of timber, then out into clear-cuts. The first viewpoint is at 1½ miles, 2200 feet. From a narrow window at midswitchback, look southwest to much-logged Eagle Creek and farther south to white peaks above Money Creek.

Skiing on through the forest, listen for the reverberating sound of a male grouse drumming for a mate. At 2 miles is a second viewpoint, perched on the corner of an open switchback. Look north for miles up Beckler River towards Jack Pass and over innumerable peaks made mighty by their snow coverings. The third viewpoint is at 3 miles, 2900 feet, just as the road levels off for its long traverse to Alpine Baldy. Cliffs above prevent ski ascents of 4950-foot Beckler Peak. Below and to the south are Tye and Foss Rivers, Tonga Ridge, Maloney microwave tower, Sobieski Mountain, and beyond them, Mt. Hinman and Mt. Daniels.

Past the third viewpoint the road traverses, losing 120 feet in 1½ miles, then regaining it on Alpine Baldy. Views extend over Deception and Martin creeks to Windy Mountain. From the road-end at 4200 feet an abandoned spur road may be followed up a shoulder to the 4400-foot level on Alpine Baldy. Skiers with mountaineer-level skills may continue up open slopes to the summit at 5200 feet.

83

Skyline Lake

29 HEATHER RIDGE

Skill level advanced
Round trip 4 miles
Skiing time 3 hours
Elevation gain 1200 feet
High point 5200 feet
Best January–March
Avalanche potential low
USGS Stevens Pass and Labyrinth

Map—page 85

Years before skinny skis, refugees from the mobs at the Stevens Pass Ski Area were fleeing across the highway to untracked slopes of Heather Ridge. Though the long, south-facing ascent rarely offered the far-famed

"Stevens powder," and explorers were burdened by heavy mountaineering outfits, they returned time and time again. Nowadays Heather Ridge is an extremely popular tour for advanced skiers. The reason is the same now as it was then—views over miles and miles of white-topped peaks.

Drive Highway 2 to the summit of Stevens Pass and park on the north side in the downhill lot, elevation 4050 feet. Scramble up the snowbank behind the gas station and follow a cat road to the left. Pass a cluster of vacation cottages on the right and follow an old service road through the trees to a telephone relay station at the foot of the open slopes.

To the right of the building a primitive road, obscured by snow, heads steeply up; climbing skins are very helpful. A quarter of the way to the ridge top the road fades away somewhere under the snow. Switchback onward; in unstable conditions stay to the left (west) side of the hill.

At 4900 feet, by a radio relay shed, the hard climbing ends and Mt. Hinman and Mt. Daniel come in view. However, the really big picture awaits above. Ski northwest just below the heavy timber, then turn uphill in thinning forest to the snow plain of Skyline Lake, 5092 feet. Continue to the base of a rock knob on the ridge crest. Unless equipped with ice ax, do not try for the top; be satisfied with the superb view from the saddle including Glacier Peak to the north and Mt. Stuart to the southeast.

Warm up for the steep descent by trying some of the short slopes around Skyline Lake.

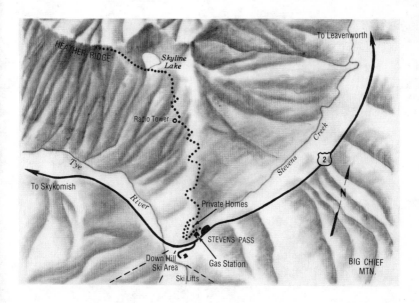

30 MILL CREEK

MILL CREEK ROAD	LANHAM LAKE
Skill level basic and up	Skill level advanced
Round trip to road-end 8 miles	Round trip 3½ miles
Skiing time 5 hours	Skiing time 4 hours
Elevation gain 500 feet	Elevation gain 1200 feet
High point 3500 feet	High point 4200 feet
Best December–March	Best December–March
Avalanche potential low	Avalanche potential none
USGS Labyrinth and Stevens Pass	USGS Labyrinth

Map—page 87

Mill Creek offers a sort of valley tour unusual for the Cascades, not through deep forest but out in the open with broad vistas of surrounding peaks. Skiers of all levels find the scene uniquely appealing. Unfortunately, so do the snowmobilers. The advanced skier can escape them on a challenging ascent to Lanham Lake.

Drive Highway 2 east 5.8 miles beyond Stevens Pass to the Sno-Park on the eastbound lane; an access road gives entry from the westbound lane. Elevation, 2800 feet.

Ski up Mill Creek road, which climbs moderately 1½ miles, then levels in the wide-open spaces with unlimited views and roaming—and machinery. Follow powerlines the next 2½ miles to the road-end, passing many picnic spots.

From the road-end, 4 miles from the Sno-Park, ambitious skiers, during stable conditions, can follow powerlines 1200 feet up to the Pacific

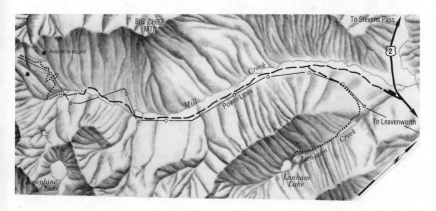

Lanham Lake and Jim Hill Mountain

Crest Trail and proceed either north to Stevens Pass Ski Area or south to Lake Susan Jane.

To escape man's trammeling and find peace, beauty, and excellent skiing, aim for Lanham Lake. Leave the valley road on the first spur to the left; at about 1 mile from the Sno-Park it leads up and back to the powerlines. Ski along these until the slope drops off just above Lanham Creek, and turn uphill into the trees. Once away from the buzzing and humming of the powerlines (one wonders what the electricity is doing to one's blood, and bones, and brains), cross several old logging roads. Keep left, staying within 500 feet of the creek, traversing open meadows where the works of man are out of sight, hearing, and mind. The valley narrows, the walls close in, and a scant ½ mile of steep climbing leads to Lanham Lake, 4143 feet. Nestled in the trees, the serenely frozen lake offers many fine picnic and camp spots with safe views up to icicled ramparts of 6765-foot Jim Hill Mountain.

NASON CREEK

31 COULTER SKI TRAIL

Skill level advanced ·
One-way to road-end 6½ miles
Skiing time 6 hours
Elevation gain 2800 feet
High point 5000 feet
Best March–April
Avalanche potential low
USGS Wenatchee Lake and
Chiwaukum Mountains

Map — page 90

Trailside snack

The Coulter Ski Trail gives access to several days of excellent skiing in the Chiwaukum Mountains. Open, rolling slopes and forested ridges often covered with deep powder, heart-catching vantage points with almost daily sunbreaks, and miles of marked ski trails are just some of the attractions.

The approach is long and requires careful navigation through a complex system of logging roads. There are two good ways. The first is to follow the Coulter Ski Trail marked and maintained by the Starks, owner-operators of the Scottish Lakes cross-country ski resort, but freely open to everyone. The second choice, many say the first, is to ride the Starks' snow-cat — or at least send the packs on it — to their 5000-foot

Overlooking Coulter and Nason Creek valleys

Nomad Ski Camp, saving time and energy for the better skiing above. Visitors may even leave their tent at home and stay in the camp's heated tent cabins. For further information contact Bill and Peg Stark, P.O. Box 303, Leavenworth, Washington 98826.

Drive Highway 2 east of Stevens Pass 17 miles. Just opposite the Rest Area, closed in winter, turn off the highway onto the Coulter Creek road system, elevation 2200 feet.

This area is privately owned. The plowing is privately paid for and parking is limited. Please do not block other cars or driveways. Unless a Sno-Park can be established (maybe in the Rest Area), during heavy snow be prepared to park as far away as Leavenworth and hitchhike back. Occasionally parking is available .1 mile west, one road past the state gravel pit. Be sure to keep a shovel handy to dig out if it snows.

Starting from the railroad tracks, walk the first ¼ mile to a signed junction and turn right on the Coulter Ski Trail. Another ¼ mile brings a left turn at a large Y, 2300 feet. As the way climbs, stay left, then go right at the next two intersections. At 1¾ miles enter the base of a clearcut. Ascend to the left, avoiding the cliffs. After gaining 200 feet, head up the clearcut, aiming for the upper right side. Crest the top of a ridge, 3900 feet, to find a road and tremendous views west to the Chiwaukums and east to Nason Ridge. Bear left, losing a few hundred feet to a three-way intersection at 3 miles.

Turn up, following the cat tracks past Starks' Midway Camp and

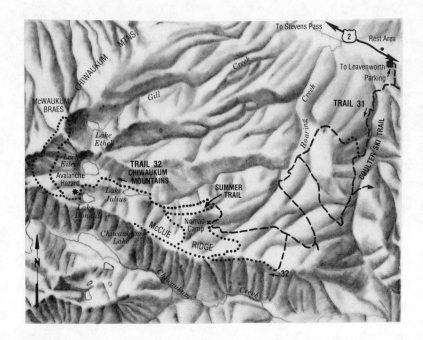

marked ski trails. At 6½ miles, 5000 feet, is Nomad Ski Camp, the end of the Coulter Ski Trail but just the start of the good skiing. Either stay with the Starks or at one of the many excellent campsites to be found in the forest beyond and spend several days exploring this vast skiers' paradise.

NASON CREEK

32 CHIWAUKUM MOUNTAINS (SCOTTISH LAKES)

Skill level intermediate and up
Over 20 miles of trails
Skiing time 1–5 days
Elevation gain 100–1500 feet
High point 7000 feet
Best January–mid-May
Avalanche potential low
USGS Wenatchee Lake and Chiwaukum Mountains

Map—page 90

Miles of open hills, forested ridge tops, checkerboard meadows, and frozen lakes combine to offer some of the most exhilarating skiing in the Cascades. There are marked ski trails and untouched wilderness, short

Lake Julius below the McWaukum Braes

forest loops and long high-country treks in the Scottish Lakes area of the Chiwaukum Mountains.

On Highway 2 between Stevens Pass and Leavenworth, just opposite the Rest Area, find the road signed "Lake Julius." Only a very few feet along a logging road are available for parking, and skiers in midwinter must be prepared to cope with this problem.

Getting into the area requires at least one day. Either ski up the Coulter Ski Trail or make reservations with the Starks (Trail 31) for snow-cat transport to their Nomad Ski Camp at 5000 feet. If not staying at Nomad Camp, follow the ridge towards Lake Julius and choose from among the numerous campsites along the ridge, Roaring Creek valley below, or at Loch Eileen. The Starks have laid out and marked a number of ski trails for all degrees of skill and energy. The trips all begin at Nomad Camp.

Skiing on McCue Ridge is especially delightful after a fresh snowfall

A shorty, for the fun of it, is the Humpity Bumpity Ski Trail, a 1-hour romp.

Serious backcountry skiers will be unable to resist the formidable all-day trip up the McWaukum Braes. From the end of the Coulter Ski Trail ski the Summer Trail along the ridge above Roaring Creek for 1½ miles, then descend to the valley ½ mile below Lake Julius. Head east up the valley, passing Lake Julius to the north. Shortly beyond the lake follow the valley as it makes an abrupt turn to the north. Climb 500 feet in 1 mile to Loch Eileen.

Above Loch Eileen, head east, climbing steeply. This short section has the only avalanche potential in the area and should not be done in unstable conditions. At the top of the narrow ledge, go right, skiing above the 5900-foot Lake McDonald. From here, the skiing is open to the top of any of the three braes.

McCue Ridge is another excellent run. The trip through forest and meadows is marked for the whole 2½ miles of ridge crest and along several of the access trails. It can be skied in all weather conditions but is best on a sunny day when views from a 6258-foot viewpoint extend for miles over the whole Chiwaukum Range.

33 LAKE WENATCHEE STATE PARK

Skill level basic and up
Loop trip 6 miles
Skiing time 4 hours
Elevation gain 130 feet
High point 2000 feet
Best January–mid-March
Avalanche potential none
USGS Plain

Map—page 93

From silent forest to lake waters enlivened by reflections of snow-covered Nason, Wenatchee, and Poe ridges, the rolling terrain around the south entrance to Lake Wenatchee State Park is popular among local skiers. Especially appealing is the fact that snow machines, which "own" the rest of the area including the north section of the park, are not allowed here.

Drive Highway 2 east 19 miles from Stevens Pass and turn left 3.6 miles on Highway 207 to Lake Wenatchee. Turn left again at the south entrance to Lake Wenatchee State Park, cross Nason Creek, then stay

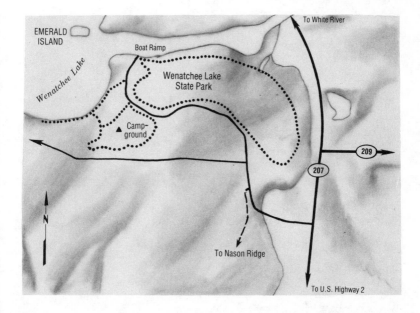

right as the road splits. Drive to the lakeshore and park, elevation 1870 feet.

The loop starts from the boat ramp and heads up right on a trail groomed regularly by park personnel and once a year by the Leavenworth Ski Club for their marathon race. The direction and length vary somewhat from year to year; in years of very heavy snowfall the trail through dense timber has to be essentially let go because of deep tree wells. The way winds through the campground area, generally crisscrossed with tracks of rabbits and small rodents—and of the coyotes and local dogs that pursue them.

A second option, shorter and very scenic, is to follow the shore around the west end of the lake. Start from the restroom near the lakeshore and ski along the lake edge. In good weather Poe Ridge and Dirtyface Peak cast gleaming white reflections on the blue waters. Private homes put an end to this peaceful tour at 1½ miles. The return may be lengthened by adding a loop up into the campground.

Dirtyface Peak and Lake Wenatchee

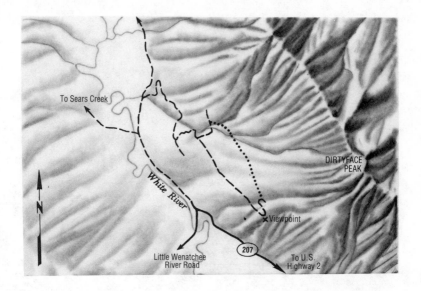

To Sears Creek

White River

N

DIRTYFACE PEAK

× Viewpoint

Little Wenatchee River Road

207

To U.S. Highway 2

LAKE WENATCHEE

34 WHITE RIVER VIEWPOINT

Skill level basic and up
Round trip to viewpoint 10 miles
Skiing time 6 hours
Elevation gain 900 feet
High point 2880 feet
Best January–mid-April
Avalanche potential none
USGS Lake Wenatchee

Map—page 95

From a vantage point atop sheer cliffs on the side of Dirtyface Peak, look out over the meandering Little Wenatchee River as it enters Lake Wenatchee, then up to formidable Nason Ridge in its warlike armor of snow, Wenatchee Ridge to the west, and the scholarly Poet Peaks beyond. On the way to and from the viewpoint, Glacier Peak puts the finishing touch on the northern horizon.

The vantage point is the highlight of a 5-mile ski. The first 3 miles along the White River road are nearly level and skiable by all skill levels. The final 2 miles are up a well-maintained logging road, best for skiers of at least intermediate level. On the return trip advanced and mountaineer

Nason Ridge from the White River viewpoint

skiers may make a cross-country loop through heavy timber, a challenge not only to skiing but to routefinding ability.

Drive Highway 2 east from Stevens Pass 19 miles and turn left toward Lake Wenatchee on road No. 207. Pass the Lake Wenatchee State Park, the road to Plain, and another to Fish Lake. At 13.5 miles from Highway 2 turn right on the White River road. Park in .2 mile at the end of the plowed road, elevation 1920 feet.

The White River road tends to be rutted and often icy. It receives considerable snowmobile use by homeowners in addition to recreationists. However, the ski up the valley is beautiful, bounded by steep flanks of 6240-foot Dirtyface Peak and Wenatchee Ridge.

At 3 miles, ¼ mile past the Sears Creek cutoff, turn right and head uphill, following the viewpoint signs. At the top of a large clearcut take a breather and gaze up the White River towards 7420-foot Mt. David, with Glacier Peak beyond. Pass two partially overgrown spur roads, the first on the right and the second on the left, to reach the viewpoint at 5 miles, 2880 feet. To the south Round Mountain, Alpine, and Mt. Mastiff are strung together by Nason Ridge. To the west are the patchy clearcuts on Wenatchee Ridge. Below are flat plains where the Little Wenatchee and White rivers flow into Lake Wenatchee. Unless you have 8-foot skis stay back from the edge—it's a long ski jump to the bottom.

A short loop may be made by continuing up past the viewpoint. The road, partially overgrown from here on, ends in ½ mile. From there head off left through the trees, descending north along a series of benches to reach a deep gully. Cross to the other side and follow the gully (with creek, if flowing) down to intersect the second of the two spur roads passed on the way up. Ski down the spur to the viewpoint road to close the 2-mile loop.

LAKE WENATCHEE

35 FLYING LOOP

Skill level intermediate and up
Loop trip 5 miles
Skiing time 3 hours
Elevation gain 680 feet
High point 2590 feet
Best December–February
Avalanche potential none
USGS Plain

Map—page 98

A pleasant ridge top, surprising viewpoints, challenging terrain, and skiers-only trails make this a unique area in the middle of the Chiwawa snow-machine country. However, be forewarned; the trail was named

High point of the Flying Loop Trail

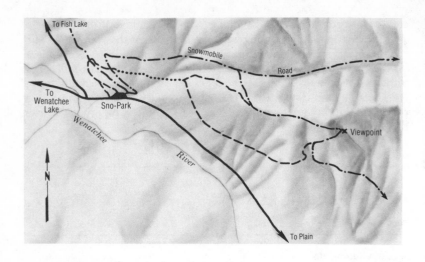

Flying Loop Trail is mostly forested

for the most common mode of descent—the "flying loop."

From Highway 2 between Stevens Pass and Leavenworth turn north towards Lake Wenatchee on Highway 207. Pass the state park turnoff to a Y at 4.5 miles. Keep right, passing Fish Lake road and Midway, 1.6 miles to the Sno-Park, elevation 1970 feet. At the lower southwest corner find the Flying Loop Ski Trail, marked with blue diamonds.

The ski trail sets out northwest, starting gently upward on an old logging road. In ¼ mile cross a groomed snowmobile trail. In ½ mile cross a second snowmobile trail and head up into the trees, away from the machines. In 1 mile the ski trail reaches a junction and the beginning of the loop. To avoid collisions on the narrow trail ahead, the Forest Service recommends going clockwise (left).

In the next 1¼ miles the trail climbs to a ridge top, 2590 feet, then traverses it ½ mile. A short descent leads to a viewpoint at the southern end of the ridge. From this high perch of 2580 feet the scenery is sublime. Below are Plain valley, the gleaming Wenatchee River, and a corner of the lake. To the southwest are the Chiwaukum Mountains, to the west the white, shining Cascades. Unfortunately, the ridge must be shared with nonskiers who have little time for the scenery, busy as they are making speed and noise on their machines.

At 2¼ miles the descent from the ridge begins with the "flying loop." If the trail ahead looks too formidable, retrace your steps to the Sno-Park. The descent is rapid as the trail drops into forest in a series of switchbacks and then goes west around the hill on a rolling traverse.

At 4 miles the loop is closed and the final mile takes you back over your own tracks to the Sno-Park.

---

36 LEAVENWORTH

Skill level basic and up
10 miles of groomed trails
Skiing time 1–2 days
Elevation gain 200 feet
High point average elevation 1200 feet
Best January–mid-March
Avalanche potential none
USGS Leavenworth

Map—page 101

Ski beautifully groomed tracks over open fields, skim along banks of the Wenatchee River, or rollercoaster up and down through ponderosa pine forest at the base of Tumwater Mountain—all in the countryside around the town of Leavenworth.

An active cross-country ski club in Leavenworth keeps three trails groomed; a small donation is asked to help keep the grooming machines running. Skiers of all levels find appropriate challenges in the set tracks: Beginners find them an asset in keeping the boards going in the right direction; intermediates practice technique without worrying about becoming lost or having the encumbrance of a pack; advanced skiers work on stride and ski for time.

Golf Course. The most popular area is the golf course. At the west edge of Leavenworth turn south off Highway 2 on Icicle road. Drive .6 mile to the Golf Course road and turn left on it .1 mile to the end.

There are two loops. The outer loop, most suitable for beginners, circles the course in about 2 miles. The inner loop is about 1 mile longer and requires good control on the hills.

Fish Hatchery. South of Highway 2, 2.1 miles on Icicle road turn left on Hatchery road .3 mile to the hatchery. Park in front of the main buildings and walk to the road-end.

Ski trails—only occasionally groomed—head south along the levee on the hatchery side of Icicle Creek and circle through forest, fields, and a housing development. The terrain is mostly level, good for families.

Leavenworth Ski Hill. Near the west end of town turn north on Ski Hill Drive 1.4 miles up through orchards to the winter sports area. Just inside the gate starts a 1½ mile, regularly groomed loop. This is the most challenging of the three trails, going up and down and winding around the rolling hills.

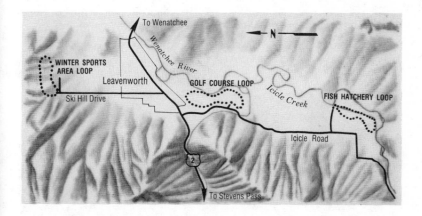

Paralleling the Wenatchee River on the Golf Course Loops

37 BESSEMER MOUNTAIN

Skill level advanced
Round trip 8 miles
Skiing time 4–6 hours
Elevation gain 3800 feet
High point 5000 feet
Best January–April
Avalanche potential low
USGS Mt. Baker

Map—page 103

Broad views west over Puget Sound country to Seattle and the Olympic Mountains. Close-up views of the rugged cliffs of Garfield Mountain and an aerial view of the Middle Fork Snoqualmie River valley. Most of most winters the Middle Fork road is snowfree, so except for bathtub-sized chuckholes, there usually is a good chance of driving to the trip start.

Drive Interstate 90 east past North Bend and go off on Exit 34, signed "Edgewick Road." Cross left under the freeway, pass Ken's Truck Town, and turn right on SE Middle Fork Snoqualmie River road. At 5.2 miles cross the Middle Fork and at 6.8 miles spot a prominent but unmarked

Mt. Garfield rising above the Middle Fork Snoqualmie River

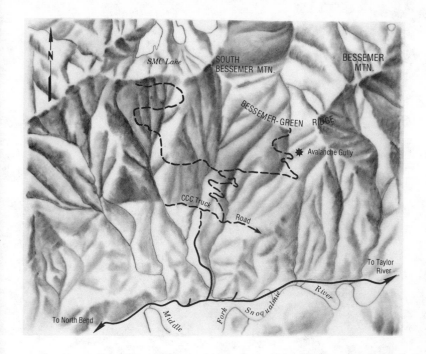

road angling up left. Watch carefully because several other unmarked roads go only a short distance. At 1 mile from the Middle Fork road reach the old CCC (Civilian Conservation Corps) Truck road, elevation 1277 feet. This is the base point for the trip, since washouts often halt driving here, or soon after, or even before.

Washouts permitting, however, drive to the snowline. Turn right on the CCC Truck road a scant ¼ mile to an unmarked junction and go left, uphill, in a series of switchbacks that climb relentlessly through tall second-growth forest, then short second-growth, then bare-slope clear-cuts. Views are excellent and get steadily bigger and better. At 2000 feet, 1½ miles from the 1277-foot base point, is a well-defined Y, presenting a choice. Let snow conditions make the decision.

The left fork climbs 2½ miles to a 4500-foot knoll atop the Bessemer-Green Ridge with exciting 360-degree views to go with lunch. The grade on this road is relatively gentle, suitable to a day when the snow is firm and a skier might have trouble standing up on a steeper slope.

For an even more gigantic summit view, climb the steeper right fork 2 miles to a 5000-foot flat-top promontory (bulldozed flat by the loggers!), a snowball's throw from the summit of South Bessemer Mountain. One stretch just below the promontory traverses a very steep slope that is perfect for an advanced skier when the snow is deep or sticky, but could be hazardous if icy. In such cases don't try to cross, but be satisfied with the views of the Cascades and assume it would be too hazy anyway to see Puget Sound country on the other side.

Mt. Kent from the Bandera Overlook

38 BANDERA OVERLOOK

Skill level intermediate and up
Round trip to overlook 5 miles
Skiing time 3 hours
Elevation gain 885 feet
High point 2485 feet
Best January-February
Avalanche potential low
USGS Bandera

Map—page 105

When the snow level descends from mountain passes to the lowlands of Puget Sound and roads could serve as championship skating rinks, the Bandera Overlook, near the edge of the Cascades, is usually accessible. The overlook, a flat promontory ideal for lunch and a little early-season sunbathing, stands high above the South Fork Snoqualmie River. From river and freeway and snow-covered valley the eye rises to a skyline of ridges and peaks. When the snow level jumps back up to the lofty heights, there is still good skiing on Mason Lake Way, an alternate road leading to views.

Drive Interstate 90 east from North Bend 14.9 miles and go off on Exit 45, signed "Bandera Airport." Park only in the Sno-Park on the south side of the freeway. *Do not* park in the interchange area.

The trip starts on the north side of Interstate 90 on a forest road. The first ½ mile parallels the freeway to a major junction. (Straight ahead is Mason Lake Way, which does not go to the lake.) For the overlook bear right on road No. 9030.

The road climbs steadily for a mile through heavy forest which opens up to reveal Mt. Gardner and a frozen-looking McClellan Butte. At 2 miles Granite Mountain appears to the northeast. Stripped of trees as it

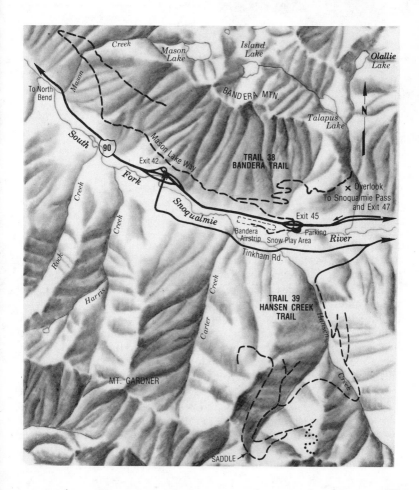

is, there would seem to be great skiing on the open slopes, but extremely high avalanche danger makes it a better mountain to just look at.

The main road ends at the overlook. If time remains after trying to name all the peaks and drainages from McClellan Butte to the backside of the Snoqualmie ski areas, continue east another ½ mile. The way becomes brushy and narrow and is skied for fun rather than views.

When the snow level is higher than Interstate 90, drive as far as possible on Mason Lake Way, then ski on up the road to the open slopes under Bandera Mountain, with views rivaling those from the overlook.

SOUTH FORK SNOQUALMIE RIVER

39 HANSEN CREEK

Skill level intermediate and up
Round trip 2–15 miles
Skiing time 2–8 hours
Elevation gain up to 2693 feet
High point 4693 feet
Best March–May
Avalanche potential low
USGS Bandera

Map—page 105

Open slopes in the upper Hansen Creek Valley

Throughout the winter the Hansen Creek area is inaccessible for all practical purposes, due to the lack of parking and high avalanche potential. In spring, however, there are valleys, ridge tops, clearcuts, and miles of logging roads to explore on skis—and miles and miles of green valleys and white mountains to look at.

Drive Interstate 90 east from North Bend. Go off on Exit 47 and turn right on Asahel Curtis-Tinkham road .2 mile to a T intersection and the end of pavement. Take the right fork 1.3 miles and turn left on Hansen Creek road No. 5510, which climbs steadily west .8 mile to a wide turn-out on the left, elevation 2000 feet. Park here or at the snowline.

From the parking area the road turns abruptly south, entering Hansen Creek valley and crossing under a tall, spindly train trestle. At 1.1 miles pass a spur to the left and in a long ½ mile more, a second spur. Beyond the second intersection the road levels off in the upper valley and enters clearcuts. Views begin, starting with Bandera Mountain to the north. Stay on the main road as it crosses Hansen Creek at 2 miles, 2900 feet,

Granite Mountain

and swing around onto a side valley; Granite Mountain comes in view, to the east of Bandera. At 3 miles cross an unnamed tributary of Hansen Creek and reach a major junction. Take the left fork, heading up the valley. From this point the choice of objectives should be made by available time and energy.

The saddle at the end of the valley is the closest of many good turn-arounds. Follow the road as it curves left around the valley head and take the first right back to the ridge top, 3900 feet, at 5½ miles. Gaze southeast over the Cedar River valley, source of Seattle's water.

From the saddle there are two possibilities, north or south. The south leads to good downhill skiing in clearcuts and at 2 miles to a 4693-foot knoll with views of Rainier, Cedar River, and McClellan Butte. Ski the approach road back ½ mile, then ascend to the top right corner of a large clearcut. A short passage through trees emerges in another clearcut just below the summit.

North from the saddle the road provides views over the South Fork Snoqualmie, from the ribbon-like freeway in the valley up to rugged summits of Snoqualmie Pass peaks. At 1½ miles the road ends in views that include Mt. Gardner, Bandera Mountain, and Mt. Defiance.

40 COLD CREEK

TWIN LAKES TRAILHEAD

Skill level basic and up
Round trip to trailhead 6 miles
Skiing time 4 hours
Elevation gain 360 feet
High point 3100 feet
Best January–April
Avalanche potential low
USGS Snoqualmie Pass

MT. CATHERINE LOOP

Skill level advanced
Loop trip 8 miles
Skiing time 5 hours
Elevation gain 1360 feet
High point 4000 feet
Best January–April
Avalanche potential low
USGS Snoqualmie Pass

Map—page 108

The Cold Creek valley behind Pacific West Ski Resort at Snoqualmie Pass has several features that make it unique: The area is suitable for beginners, offering them views over Keechelus Lake and a secluded sub-alpine valley as a destination; there is no snowmobile competition; the area is watched over by a nordic ski patrol; and finally, a loop trip around Mt. Catherine challenges the most expert skier.

Drive Interstate 90 east 1.4 miles beyond Snoqualmie Pass and go off

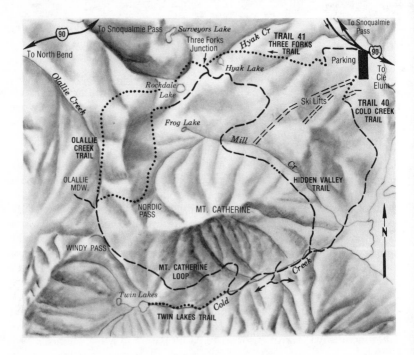

Keechelus Lake

on Rocky Run Exit 54. The Pacific West Ski Resort (Hyak) has made parking available in their lot for a fee.

Lake and loop trips start off together on the far southeast side of the ski area, elevation 2640 feet. Climb above the rope tow to the road, which begins directly below a chalet perched on the side of the hill and maintains a constant elevation as it traverses left through timber. Within ½ mile of the ski area is an overlook of Keechelus Lake and Mt. Margaret to the northeast. At 1 mile the road turns inland and heads up Cold Creek. For the next 2 miles the road climbs gently but steadily up Cold Creek. The Hidden Valley tour (Trail 41) drops from the upper ski area to intersect the road on the right at 2¾ miles. At 3 miles, 2960 feet, the road switchbacks; advanced and mountaineer level skiers may leave the main road and go straight ahead on unmarked trail ¾ mile, first in forest across the bottom of a big clearcut and finally back in forest to Twin Lakes. This is a recommended objective only when the avalanche hazard is low.

To do the loop make the switchback to stay on the main road, where gaining elevation becomes the prime order of business. Pass a deadend spur at 3½ miles and reach aptly named Windy Pass at 4½ miles, 3800 feet. The route beyond here is marked by blue diamonds; however, they often are obscure, so be sure to carry a map. At the pass leave the road as it emerges from a narrow strip of trees. Head right, dropping 160 feet of elevation to the head of Olallie Meadows. Bear right, cross the top end of the meadows, then climb steeply east to Nordic Pass, a short ¼ mile, 4000 feet. Staying on route through dense timber now becomes a challenge. Keep on the left (north) side of the valley to a logging road at 5½ miles, 3700 feet. Follow the road around Rockdale Lake to Three Forks Junction. Close the loop by descending Three Forks Trail (Trail 41) to the parking lot.

41 THREE FORKS TRAILS

Skill level intermediate and up
Round trip 6–12 miles
Skiing time 4–8 hours
Elevation gain up to 1100 feet
High point 3700 feet
Best January–April
Avalanche potential low
USGS Snoqualmie Pass

Map—page 108

Tucked away behind the downhill ski areas of Snoqualmie Pass lies easily accessible high country excellent for Nordic skiing. Just out of sight and barely out of sound of the tow-hill scene is the hidden world of cross-country skiers with steep open slopes, gently rolling hills, lakes, meadows, forests, and breathtaking views. The Forest Service, in co-operation with Pacific West Ski Resort (Hyak), has built an extensive system of ski trails.

Drive Interstate 90 east of Snoqualmie Pass and go off on Exit 54 to the parking lot at Pacific West Ski Resort, elevation 2640 feet.

Pacific West traditionally has been very receptive to cross-country skiing guests. A complete Nordic ski shop provides everything from rentals to waxes and maps. There is free parking for skiers renting skis at the shop; others may be charged a fee.

There are three good ways to the high meadows. The first is Three Forks Trail. From the parking lot ski up the right side of the ski area towards a group of winter chalets and find a road that winds through them. At 3000 feet, opposite a large cylinder painted as a beer can, the trail starts. Turn right into the trees, traversing north. Just before a powerline clearing, head uphill following blue diamonds in a long series of switchbacks. Near the top the trail heads west, rounding Hyak Lake at 3500 feet, to reach Three Forks Junction at 3 mile, 3600 feet.

The second way to get to the top or back down is Hidden Valley Trail. Follow Cold Creek Trail (Trail 40) 2¾ miles to 2800 feet, turn right and follow logging roads through a wide clearcut with a view of Keechelus Lake and Mt. Margaret. From the road follow the powerlines up Mill Creek behind Mt. Hyak. Once up, ski across the rolling countryside to Three Forks Junction at 4 miles.

The third method is to ride the chairlift up and then follow a downhill run right to a saddle, 3420 feet. Continue on straight, northwest, from the saddle, leaving the downhill slopes for a quiet mile on a logging spur to Three Forks Junction.

From Three Forks Junction skiers may branch out over rolling hills of the vast snow-play area or explore the "three forks." The left fork comes from the lifts and Hidden Valley Trail. The middle fork is part of the Mt. Catherine Loop (Trail 40). A ½-mile cruise over this trail passes timber-ringed Rockdale Lake. The right fork leads over logging road and then trail 2 miles to Olallie Meadows, adjacent to clearcuts with views that extend far down the South Fork Snoqualmie River. Good skiing and sheltered campsites may be found here. From the meadows, skiers may follow Cold Creek road back to the parking lot or the Mt. Catherine Loop back to Three Forks Junction (Trail 40).

Skiers near Three Forks Junction

Information board at Rocky Run Sno-Park keeps skiers posted on daily avalanche hazard

---

KEECHELUS LAKE

42 KENDALL PEAK ROAD

Skill level intermediate and up
Round trip 6½ miles
Skiing time 4 hours
Elevation gain 1700 feet
High point 4400 feet
Best December–April
Avalanche potential moderate
USGS Snoqualmie Pass

Map—page 114

Open slopes or logging roads are the options in this versatile area near Snoqualmie Pass. Kids can leave their parents on the downhill slopes (or vice versa) and head out for cross-country skiing just across the valley, there to enjoy—on a clear day—views over miles of gleaming mountains, and on any day very cheap lift tickets, costing only one's own energy supplied by granola bars.

Drive Interstate 90 east from Snoqualmie Pass 1.4 miles and go off on Rocky Run Exit 54. Park in the Sno-Park on the north side of the freeway along the plowed section of the old highway, elevation 2640 feet. Check the Forest Service information board in the parking area for route changes and avalanche hazard.

Kendall Peak road begins at the information board and heads north up the Gold Creek valley in conjunction with the Gold Creek Loops (Trail 43). In ⅛ mile the road turns uphill to start the climb. At ½ mile the route forks. The Gold Creek Loops go right; Kendall Peak road switchbacks left up a clearcut. Beyond the valley the downhill slopes are clearly visible, little dots shooting down the many runs.

Two major spur roads are passed, the first on the right and the second on the left as the main road turns abruptly and steeply right. Peaks south of the pass begin to pop up, dwarfing the ski areas. Such familiar summits as Mt. Catherine and Silver Peak take on new dimensions as snow exaggerates each contour; they seem not to belong here at all, but in Alaska or the Himalaya. Near the top of the clearcut a viewpoint gives a look up Gold Creek to massive rock walls of Alta Mountain and Chikamin Ridge.

At 2 miles, 3600 feet, the road enters forest; briefly one can visualize Snoqualmie Pass before it was logged, groomed, and tamed. In ¼ mile the way emerges from trees to the base of another clearcut. When snow is unstable, the steep, open slopes above the road may slide. In these conditions retreat to the lower hills. In stable conditions ski up the road 1

Snoqualmie Pass downhill ski areas viewed from Kendall Peak road

more mile to the end at 4400 feet on Kendall Knob to a flat landing, a good picnic spot.

Advanced or mountaineer skiers may make a scenic sidetrip from the knob to the snowbound Kendall Peak Lakes. Ski back across the flat-topped knob until the terrain starts to rise. Climb two short rises, then traverse north to the stream drainage and turn uphill to the lowest lake, 4360 feet, a short ½ mile from the knob. The second Kendall Peak Lake, a short ¼ mile up the valley, is the turnaround. There is serious avalanche hazard beyond.

The return from the knob can be made in a steep nonstop slide down the clearcuts. However, when avalanche hazard is high, stay on the road until the lower clearcut is reached.

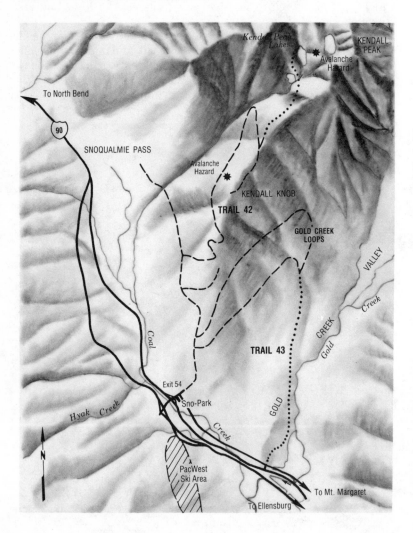

Shoulder of Kendall Peak from Gold Creek Valley

43 GOLD CREEK VALLEY

Skill level basic and up
Round trips up to 6 miles
Skiing time 2-4 hours
Elevation gain 200 feet
High point 2900 feet
Best January-March
Avalanche potential low
USGS Snoqualmie Pass

Map—page 114

Gold Creek valley, just east of Snoqualmie Pass, is one of the state's most popular learning areas for cross-country skiers. The low rolling hills and wide-open valley floor are ideal for everything from the basic stride to the telemark. Moreover, the education takes place amid breathtaking mountain scenery.

Drive Interstate 90 east from Snoqualmie Pass 2 miles and go off on Rocky Run Exit 54. Park in the Sno-Park on the north side of the freeway, elevation 2640 feet.

There are two marked ski loops and miles of valley to explore. The marked loops start from the information board and head up the valley on a Forest Service road. In ¼ mile turn uphill and climb about 200 feet in ¼ mile in conjunction with the Kendall Peak road (Trail 42). At the first major junction go right and follow blue diamonds down a rough spur road back to the valley floor and across the open plain. The loop enters the trees, follows a series of narrow roads, and ends in a steep descent at the log-scaling station .3 mile east of the starting point.

Don't be surprised if you get lost; it happens to most skiers in this area because the Forest Service placed only a minimum of markers, in compliance with wishes of private developers who own most of the land.

The most rewarding Gold Creek experience is to forget marked trails and simply explore. Ski along the creek and wonder at the large amount of water that flows from the frozen mountains above. Contrast twisted old silver snags to living counterparts. Slide across open meadows in view of the snow-plastered rock faces of Alta Mountain and Chikamin Ridge. Skiers wishing to penetrate deep into the valley should start on the east side of Gold Creek to avoid the large hummocks and streams of the west side. On either side do not ski beyond 2½ miles; avalanche potential is extreme in upper reaches of the valley.

The Forest Service hopes to move the Sno-Park .3 mile east to the scaling station and from it to develop a network of trails, greatly increasing the cross-country fun in Gold Creek.

Gold Creek is a popular area for beginner to expert skiers

44 MT. MARGARET

Skill level intermediate and up
Round trip to false summit 9 miles
Skiing time 5 hours
Elevation gain 2880 feet
High point 5440 feet
Best January–mid-April
Avalanche potential low
USGS Snoqualmie Pass

Map—page 118

The west side of Mt. Margaret offers open slopes that compare to the best downhill ski areas in length and variety. A day may be spent making challenging runs down the clearcut hillside or climbing to the rugged ridge just below the summit of Mt. Margaret to enjoy the extraordinary views.

Drive Interstate 90 east from Snoqualmie Pass 2 miles to Rocky Run Exit 54. Go under the freeway to the north side and turn right at the Gold Creek Sno-Park. Drive .8 mile and park near the end of the plowed road, elevation 2560 feet. This is still part of the Sno-Park area so be sure to have a permit.

The first section parallels the freeway east along Keechelus Lake 2 miles. After passing several summer homes, the road turns uphill into timber and sets about the serious business of gaining elevation.

Near the end of the first mile of climbing, the road enters open clearcuts. Skiers may choose either to stay on the road or to leave it and strike out over the rolling slopes. An abrupt switchback at 3 miles is the scene of a possibly confusing intersection; stay right. At 3½ miles is another junction. The right fork descends gradually 6 miles to the Kachess Lake road. Take the left fork and climb steeply through an island of trees to open slopes beyond. Pass the summer parking lot for the Mt. Margaret–Lake Lillian trail, 3600 feet. After another 100 yards take a spur road on the left and head steeply uphill, following the summer route to Mt. Margaret. Once over the initial steep climb look up to the top of the clearcuts above. The objective is to reach the upper right corner either on the road or across the slopes and not be totally distracted by the terrific views, dominated by Mt. Rainier and Keechelus Lake.

From the top of the clearcut follow a logging road through a narrow band of trees to a higher clearcut. Continue on the road to the upper left corner and through another narrow band of trees overlooked by the loggers to a final clearcut and the road-end. Climb past ghost trees to the ridge top, 4800 feet, where whole new horizons extend south over miles of logged slopes to the Stampede Pass area. Intermediate-level skiers should turn around here.

The rest of the climb is in timber. Follow the crest when the going is easy, and drop a bit on the west side when the ridge is rough. Stay well away from the edge—the east side often is corniced and it's a long drop to the bottom. Several places give views to the summit and false summit.

The final ascent is up partially open slopes to the 5440-foot false summit. Taking care to stay well back from the corniced edge, gaze to the dark granite massif of Mt. Stuart. Bears Breast Mountain stands out among Dutch Miller Gap peaks. West and north are spiky peaks near Snoqualmie Pass.

The summit of Mt. Margaret lies temptingly near, but the views don't improve with the 90 extra feet of elevation and the route crosses steep slopes and giant cornices. It's best left as an excuse to return in summer.

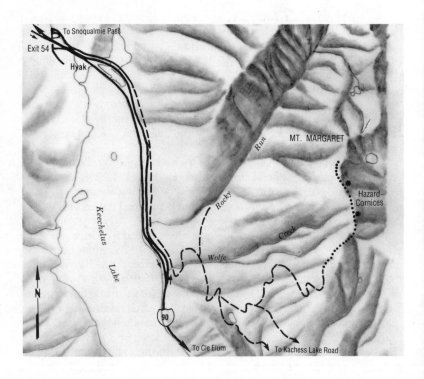

Lunch stop on the false summit of Mt. Margaret. Mt. Rainier in the distance

Keechelus Lake from Amabilis Mountain

45 AMABILIS MOUNTAIN

Skill level intermediate and up
Loop trip 8 miles
Skiing time 5 hours
Elevation gain 2154 feet
High point 4554 feet
Best January–March
Avalanche potential low
USGS Snoqualmie Pass

Map—page 122

Ski to the summit of 4554-foot Amabilis Mountain on a wide, well-graded logging road. Near the top set out on a tour more than 1½ miles along a gleaming ridge with open views of Kachess and Keechelus lakes, Stampede Pass, Mt. Catherine, Silver Peak, and above all Mt. Rainier. Make a looping return on a different logging road.

Drive Interstate 90 east from Snoqualmie Pass 10.3 miles and go off on Cabin Creek Exit 63 to the Sno-Parks on the west side of the freeway, elevation 2189 feet. Arrive early; latecomers may find the two lots full.

Cross to the north side of the freeway on the overpass to Kachess Lake road. Pass Trollhaugen Hut, a cross-country racing club; please stay off the carefully groomed tracks and avoid interference with the faster-than-a-speeding-bullet skiers. Beyond the hut the road rounds a corner and splits. Go right on Amabilis Mountain road and immediately start to climb. The way switchbacks uphill, passing several old spurs, first to the left, then to the right. Occasional windows in the forest give glimpses of massive Keechelus Ridge and the Swamp Lake area.

The first major intersection is at 2 miles, 3300 feet. This is the start of the loop and either direction will reach the top; for best enjoyment of the scenery go left. The next mile traverses into a clearcut at the north end of the mountain, switchbacks just below the ridge top, and ascends open slopes. From here on the road often is windswept and hard to follow. When visibility is poor, make the ridge top your turnaround. The final mile lies along the crest and leads, first in open clearcut then back in the trees on a logging road, to the site of an old radio tower. If the road is obscure, simply stay on the west side of the ridge to gain the summit.

For the loop return, in stable conditions only, take the road west from the beacon site, follow the forest road back to close the loop at 6 miles. This leg of the loop crosses a steep avalanche chute and should not be skied except in times of low avalanche hazard.

Skiing fresh snow on the Amabilis Mountain road

46 CABIN CREEK

CABIN CREEK LOOP	LAKE EASTON TRAIL
Skill level basic and up	Skill level basic and up
Loop trip 1 mile	One way 9½ miles
Skiing time 1 hour	Skiing time 3 hours
Elevation gain 100 feet	Elevation loss 200 feet
High point 2560 feet	High point 2450 feet
Best January–February	Best January–February
Avalanche potential none	Avalanche potential none
USGS Snoqualmie Pass	USGS Snoqualmie Pass and Kachess Lake

Map—page 122

In the midst of mountain country where all the scenery is vertical, the Cabin Creek area features valley flats and rolling hills, open and gentle terrain ideal for beginners to perfect their balance and racers to achieve speed. Two trips can be made. The first is a short, scenic loop trip that starts and ends from the parking lot. The second follows an old road to Lake Easton State Park.

Drive Interstate 90 east from Snoqualmie Pass 10.5 miles and go off on Cabin Creek Exit 63. Park in the large Sno-Park on the south side, elevation 2450 feet.

Cabin Creek Loop. The loop trip starts from the lower end of the Sno-Park and returns to the upper end. Follow the sign towards a viewpoint, leaving the parking lot on the right (west) side. Descend gently through

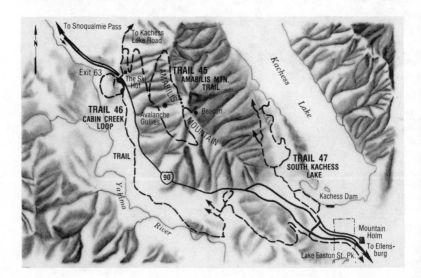

Cabin Creek Loop

second-growth to open meadows. Stay right at the first intersection. (Skiers may also enjoy a sidetrip cruise out in the meadows.) At all inter-sections keep the small knoll on your right side. In ½ mile the Yakima River meanders by the trail, then disappears in forest. In ¼ mile more a large clearcut is crossed. Ski to the top for views east to Amabilis Moun-tain (Trail 45) and southwest to Stampede Pass.

To close the loop ski out through the lower southeast corner of the clearcut to the Sno-Park entrance.

Lake Easton Trail. The Lake Easton Trail is 9½ miles one way, follow-ing the old, old, old Snoqualmie Pass road from Cabin Creek to Lake Easton State Park. The trip requires endurance but is suitable for all levels of skiers.

Volunteer cross-country skiers worked for weeks cutting a path through a jungle of underbrush to open this road as a ski trail. Snow-mobilers have remembered, however, that before the brush grew up they used it as their route from Easton to Stampede Pass. They now are claim-ing the right to use it again and the situation is uncertain. The ski route may be moved over to the powerlines, giving the road back to the snowmobilers.

47 SOUTH KACHESS LAKE

MOUNTAIN HOLM

Skill level basic and up
6½ miles of groomed trails
Skiing time 2 hours-all day
Elevation gain 80 feet
High point 2400 feet
Best December 26-February
Avalanche potential none
USGS Easton and Kachess Lake

MARSH LOOPS

Skill level basic and up
Round trip 6 miles
Skiing time 6 hours
Elevation gain 80 feet
High point 2400 feet
Best January-February
Avalanche potential none
USGS Kachess Lake

Map—page 122

*Camp Robber with feathers
fluffed to keep warm*

Two areas near the south end of Kachess Lake have enjoyable skiing for all. Mountain Holm is ideal for the beginner, offering lessons on groomed tracks or a family outing through the serene countryside. Marsh Loop ski trails, marked by the Forest Service, ·guides the skier along the scenic lakeshore and around snow-blanketed marshes at the base of Amabilis Mountain.

Mountain Holm. Drive Interstate 90 east 16.8 miles from Snoqualmie Pass and go off on Exit 70. Cross the freeway to Sparks road and turn right .3 mile to Mountain Holm's entrance on the left, elevation 2320 feet.

Mountain Holm's day lodge provides complete cross-country ski rentals and lessons, small food service, and a great place to warm up in chilly weather. The family outing will be restful with no worries about routefinding, trail-breaking, or avalanches. A day fee helps maintain the groomed tracks.

Two loop trails are regularly groomed by Mountain Holm. A 2km (1¼-mile) loop is used mostly by beginners adjusting to skinny skis. A longer 8km (5-mile) loop wanders through the silent forest, opening to views of Kachess Ridge and Easton Ridge, where mountain goats often can be seen nimbly running about the cliffs. Take time to explore the countryside, watching for rabbits, squirrels, and raccoons—or at least for their tracks. The forest may be silent, but it is full of life.

In years to come look for more groomed trails and expanded services by Mountain Holm.

Marsh Loops. From Exit 70 turn left on Sparks road 1.2 miles to the road-end parking area, elevation 2320 feet.

Ski the well-marked Forest Service road, shared by snow machines and skiers. In ¼ mile is a junction. To the right is the lakeshore, but save this leg of the loop for the return. Continue straight along the road through deep woods. In late season small streams may melt gaping pits in the snow, inconveniences that help reduce the machine traffic.

After 1¼ miles the dense forest is left behind and another intersection is reached. Bear right and meander around the marshes and ponds, under a blanket of winter white. Look west to snowbound Amabilis Mountain. At 1½ miles more is the top of the loop, where the marshes end. Bear left (west) to rejoin the machine-skier road and close the loop at 3½ miles.

Reenter the forest, following your own tracks ½ mile to a junction. Go left (east) on a short, rolling trail to the shore of Kachess Lake and an old road that parallels the shore for ½ mile. Near the dam an opening in the trees gives access to the shore, a perfect place to pull out a sandwich and enjoy winter.

The forest trail heads southwest to rejoin the machine-skier road for the final ¼ mile to the start.

Kachess Lake

Skiing the French Cabin Creek Valley

48 FRENCH CABIN CREEK

Skill level intermediate and up
Round trip 4–14 miles
Skiing time 4 hours–2 days
Elevation gain 1336 feet
High point 3600 feet
Best March–mid-May
Avalanche potential low to moderate
USGS Kachess Lake

Map—page 127

A logging road with a number of short spurs leads to a variety of destinations and views, suitable for a good half-day workout, an all-day exploration, or an overnight up the Thorp Creek Trail. The trip is very good all winter—assuming the county road can be driven to Salmon la Sac. (In midwinter it is wise to call the Cle Elum Ranger Station to check on this.) Thanks to the Forest Service, however, the French Cabin Creek road is heavily used on weekends by speeding snowmobiles, and therefore it is best for skiers to come midweek or wait until late spring when the snowmobiles give up.

Go off Interstate 90 on Exit 80 and drive Highway 903, following signs to Salmon la Sac, passing through both Roslyn and Ronald and around Cle Elum Lake. At 12 miles from Roslyn City Hall find the French Cabin Creek road, elevation 2262 feet.

The road crosses the Cle Elum River on a concrete bridge and in ¼ mile starts climbing. In the next 2 miles the road gains 1000 feet in a series of five long switchbacks, steep enough for most skiers. To escape snowmobile ruts, the first four switchbacks can be shortcut. As the road climbs, the face of Red Mountain comes in view, seemingly towering overhead, a spectacular sight after a fresh snowfall. At 2½ miles the road levels and enters French Cabin Creek valley.

Thorp Creek Trail. Energetic skiers can do an overnight ski tour to Thorp Lake, capped by an ascent (if conditions warrant) of 5854-foot Thorp Mountain. (Mountaineer Nordic skiers can handle the peak, but most skiers are better off on alpine skis.) At 3½ miles on the main road go off right on Thorp Creek road about 1 mile to its end. Continue up the valley 3 more miles to the lake. The forest travel is not easy—but does stop the machines. If the opportunity presents itself, cross to the north side of the creek, where the going is somewhat better.

Camp at the lake in forest well away from any possible avalanche (but not under a tree topped with a mushroom of snow). Do not attempt the open slopes to the ridge unless the snow is stable.

North Peak Road. At 4 miles go off left on a logging road that climbs to clearcuts on North Peak; views are great of Red Mountain and up the Salmon la Sac valley.

Knox Creek. At 5 miles go off right on Knox Creek road and climb 2

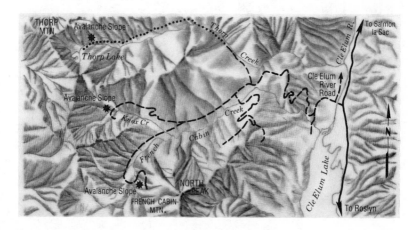

miles to the end at the foot of a large, steep mountain meadow. (Avalanche hazard is possible in the meadow.)

French Cabin Mountain. Follow the main road to its end at 7 miles in clearcuts and mountain meadows under French Cabin Mountain.

---

49 CLE ELUM RIVER

Skill level basic and up
Round trip 2–5 miles
Skiing time 1–2 hours
Elevation gain none
High point 2400 feet
Best January–March
Avalanche potential none
USGS Kachess Lake

Map—page 128

A delightful valley-bottom tour within constant sight and sound of the Cle Elum River, with a fair chance of getting away from sight and sound of snowmobiles.

The trip can either start from French Cabin Creek road (Trail 48) or

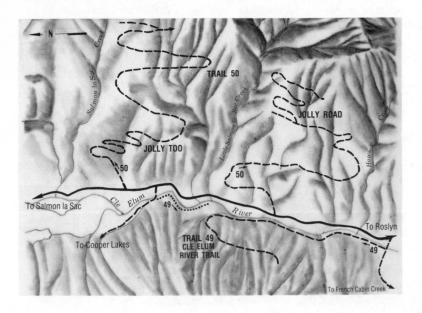

Davis Peak from the Cle Elum River

Cooper River road (Trail 51). Unfortunately, steep cliffs and the crossing of Thorp Creek make it impossible to start at one point and finish at the other.

French Cabin Creek. From French Cabin Creek road cross the Cle Elum River bridge and in ¼ mile find a spur road to the right. Follow it 2 miles to the start of the uphill—or continue 1½ miles into clearcuts and views. If there are snowmobiles, stay off the spur road and instead follow as closely as possible along the river. If snowmobiles are buzzing around and ruining your ski tracks, weave between the trees.

Cooper River Road. From Cooper River road cross the Cle Elum River on a concrete bridge and as soon as practical leave the road on the downstream side and follow as close to the river as you can. In roughly 1 mile cliffs and creeks stop progress.

50 JOLLY AND JOLLY TOO

JOLLY ROAD

Skill level basic and up
Round trip up to 8 miles
Skiing time 2–5 hours
Elevation gain up to 1720 feet
High point 4000 feet
Best January–mid-April
Avalanche potential low
USGS Kachess Lake

JOLLY TOO ROAD

Skill level basic and up
Round trip up to 7 miles
Skiing time 2–4 hours
Elevation gain up to 1800 feet
High point 4160 feet
Best January–mid-April
Avalanche potential low
USGS Kachess Lake

Map—page 128

Two fun logging roads on the east side of the Cle Elum River climb to open slopes and grand overlooks across the Cle Elum River valley up French Cabin Creek, past Red Mountain, and up Cooper River valley to Dutch Miller Gap peaks. From Jolly Too other views extend north to Davis Peak and Mt. Daniels. Because they are too short to interest snowmobilers, the roads generally are left to quieter winter travelers, although there is no official designation to insure this.

Go off Interstate 90 on Exit 80 and drive Highway 903 through the towns of Roslyn and Ronald and past Cle Elum Lake. At 14.2 miles from Roslyn City Hall park in a very small, plowed turnout on the right side of the road. There are no signs, but this is the start of Jolly road, elevation 2300 feet.

In 1 mile of gentle climbing the road gains a large bench at 2500 feet. The several-acre expanse of low, rolling bumps and flat bowls is ideal for family play. For views continue up the road another mile to the base of a large clearcut. In stable snow conditions ascend approximately 700 feet to the top of the clearcut, for the sheer joy of carving a set of turns or sitzmarks on the way back down.

Jolly Too road starts 15.4 miles from Roslyn City Hall. Park only in the small, plowed area on the right side of the road. If there is no parking space available, return .4 mile to Cooper River road and walk back.

Jolly Too road is very similar to Jolly road except a little steeper. Be sure to ski at least 2½ miles to a superb viewpoint north and west. The final 1½ miles climb towards the ridge top without ever quite getting there. However, numerous clearcuts give good skiing and tremendous views.

Jolly road

51 COOPER RIVER ROAD

Skill level intermediate and up
Round trip 5–22 miles
Skiing time 3 hours–overnight
Elevation gain 1000 feet
High point 3400 feet
Best late spring but good all winter
Avalanche potential low to moderate
USGS Kachess Lake

Map—page 133

The Cooper River road offers four different destinations, all with spectacular views of Dutch Miller Gap peaks — Lemah Mountain, Chimney Rock, Overcoat Peak, Summit Chief, and Bears Breast Mountain.

Lemah Mountain and Chimney Rock from the Cooper River road

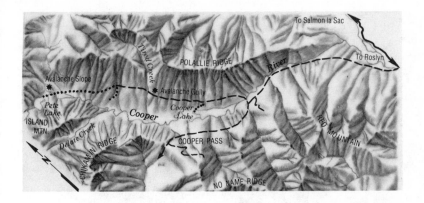

Drive from Roslyn towards Salmon la Sac (Trail 48) and 15 miles from Roslyn City Hall find Cooper River road, elevation 2400 feet.

The road is groomed for snowmobiles and generally well packed and rutted. At 4¾ miles, gaining only 300 feet, the way reaches a major junction and the four alternatives.

Cooper Lake. Go downhill right ¼ mile and cross Cooper River on a concrete bridge. Follow the road as it curves left another ¼ mile and find a spur that drops to Owhi Campground and the lakeshore, 2788 feet, 5½ miles from the beginning.

Cooper Pass. From the major junction go straight ahead, climbing clearcuts with fine views of Cooper Lake and Dutch Miller Gap peaks. At 3 miles from the junction (7¾ miles from beginning) reach Cooper Pass, 3400 feet. For better views go higher on one of the many logging roads on No Name Ridge. Cooper Pass is a great destination; unfortunately, it's great for snowmobiles also.

Tired Creek. Cross Cooper River (see Cooper Lake above), keep right at the campground-lakeshore junction, and follow the road past Tired Creek to its very end at 3400 feet, 8½ miles from the Salmon la Sac road.

This trip has excellent views of Dutch Miller Gap peaks but crosses two avalanche gullies, so don't try it for a couple of weeks after a heavy snowstorm. If the avalanches have been massive enough, they will block the snowmobiles.

Pete Lake. This is the only place in the watershed where one can get away from machines and is recommended as an overnight trip for advanced level and up. From the road-end beyond Tired Creek traverse downward in a clearcut, then forest, to the valley bottom and go upstream 2½ miles to Pete Lake and a great view of mountains (11 miles from the Salmon la Sac road). The way through the forest is not easy when the snow is so deep that there are 5-foot "wells" around trees or when it's not deep enough to bridge the half-dozen tributary streams. The route is subject to large avalanches, including an area just short of the lake.

Stuart Range viewed from the summit of Teanaway Butte

52 TEANAWAY BUTTE

Skill level intermediate and up
Round trip 15 miles
Skiing time 8 hours–2 days
Elevation gain 2129 feet
High point 4769 feet
Best March–April
Avalanche potential none
USGS Mount Stuart

Map—page 135

Ski a pristine wilderness of snow with trees laced in white and meadows under a coat of winter fluff. The final destination of Teanaway Butte gives a view that is long and wide, from Mt. Stuart north to Mt. Rainier south.

Drive Highway 970 east of Cle Elum 7.3 miles and turn left on the Teanaway River road 15.9 miles to the crossing of Lick Creek. Winter plowing stops here, so the trip is best done in spring. Drive another 4.4 miles to 29 Pines Campground and a junction. Bear left, crossing North Fork Teanaway River. In .2 mile turn left again, crossing Jungle Creek. This intersection is the start of the Rye Creek road and the base point for spring skiing, elevation 2640 feet.

Follow the road through trees and a few small, peaceful meadows. If the peacefulness is not broken by the roar of a snow machine, chances are very good of seeing deer or other wildlife. At 2½ miles pass Camp Lake, 2800 feet. The soggy marsh of summer has a whole different appearance under the crystal white of winter.

After 2 more miles of near-level travel the way turns uphill for ½ mile, then gentles again. At 5 miles, 3680 feet, is a four-way junction in a small clearing with a glimpse of Mt. Rainier, a promise of good views to come. Continue straight west to a junction at 5¾ miles, 3680 feet.

Take the right fork and head up to the northeast. As you climb through the trees bear right at the first junction and left at the second. The uphill pace becomes steep to the road-end at the base of a small knoll at 7¼ miles, 4560 feet. From here it is advised to remove skis and post-hole (leave a line of knee-deep foot holes in soft snow) the last ¼ mile and 200 feet to the top of Teanaway Butte, 4769 feet.

On this perch, far from the buzz of city life and snow machines, the views are endless. Rocky ridges of 9415-foot Mt. Stuart jab into the northern skyline. To the southeast the dormant mountain of fire and ice, Rainier, demands attention.

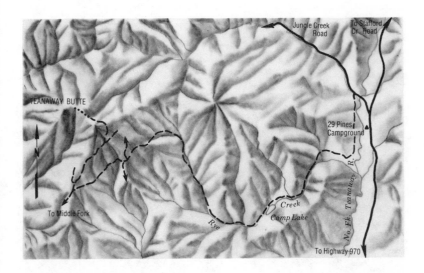

53 RED TOP MOUNTAIN LOOKOVER

Skill level intermediate and up
Round trip 17 miles
Skiing time 8 hours–2 days
Elevation gain 2480 feet
High point 5280 feet
Best January–April
Avalanche potential low
USGS Liberty and Mt. Stuart

Map—page 136

A high, open ridge gives panoramas out to Mt. Stuart, Table Mountain, Mt. Ingalls, Mt. Rainier, and the summit of Mt. Adams and down to the Swauk and Teanaway valleys. Less than ½ mile away, perched high atop a rocky fortress, is Red Top Lookout, defended against skiers by snow- and ice-covered rock. The trip is long, requiring a full day or overnight. The first 6 miles are on well-graded logging roads occasionally made noisy by snow-blitzers. The last 2½ miles are up an old skid road, then a trailless hillside, to a forested ridge top, very difficult to climb when icy.

Drive Highway 97 east of Mineral Springs (store-restaurant) .1 mile

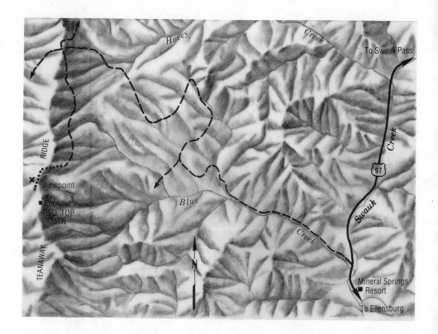

Red Top Lookout from the "Battlefield"

and turn off on road No. 2106 at Blue Creek, elevation 2800 feet, the beginning point of this trip.

At ½ mile from Highway 97, where Medicine Creek road branches left, stay right. After the first mile Red Top Lookout, high above, makes an occasional appearance.

At a major intersection, 3 miles, a sign points left to Red Top Lookout. However, for the best views—the lookover—stay right. At 6 miles is another junction at the top of a small saddle. Go left on an ill-defined skid road. Contour around the ridge to the road-end in a small, steep clearcut at 7 miles. From here climb to the ridge top. If the slope looks too steep or the snow unstable, backtrack ¼ mile to a small bend in the road and follow a gully to the ridge. Once on the crest continue south ½ mile through trees to the broad, open area of "The Battlefield," well known by the rockhounds who in summer dig pits and trenches, searching for agates. The winter restores peace, permitting skiers to serenely enjoy the views.

54 BLEWETT PASS

Skill level basic and up
Round trip 8 miles
Skiing time 4 hours
Elevation gain 1030 feet
High point 4064 feet
Best January–March
Avalanche potential low
USGS Liberty

Map—page 139

*Blewett Pass is excellent
for skiers of all levels*

Old names never die. Although Highway 97 moved from Blewett Pass to Swauk Pass over 20 years ago, the highway is still often referred to as Blewett Pass. This trip to the real Blewett Pass is full of nostalgia. When the original highway was built, Model Ts were still chugging and steaming up mountains. Since the cars weren't going fast anyhow, the old road twisted and turned its way up and over, following contours of the hillside and doubling back on itself at switchbacks. Most surprising of all is how narrow the old two-lane was.

Drive north on Highway 97 from Ellensburg or on Highway 970 from Cle Elum. At 7 miles from the junction of 97 and 970 pass Mineral Springs Resort. In 3 miles more find the old Blewett Pass Highway on the left, elevation 3048 feet. There usually is space for one or two cars to park.

The way is a gentle but steady grade up. As elevation is gained, Red Top Lookout can be seen to the southwest and the flat top of Table Mountain to the southeast. At 4 miles, 4064 feet, reach the summit of the pass. Nothing is there now, but there used to be a small restaurant and, in the late 1930s, a rope ski tow.

At the summit follow a logging road another ½ mile westward up steep slopes to broader views from clearcuts. A maze of roads offers any number of wanderings.

View from Blewett Pass

Ski trails in the Swauk Pass vicinity travel through open forest and small meadows

55 SWAUK PASS MEADOW LOOPS

Skill level basic and up
Loop trip 15 miles
Skiing time 3 hours–all day
Elevation gain up to 560 feet
High point 4400 feet
Best January–February
Avalanche potential none
USGS Liberty

Map —page 141

Deep in the heart of snowmobile country the Forest Service has reserved three short loops for travelers powered solely by cheese, bread, and peanut butter. These no-machine paths through deep forest, along old skid roads, across small meadows, over small knolls, and down steep woodland trails are sanctuaries for both skiers and wildlife.

Swauk Meadow Loop. This 4-mile loop, mostly forested except for a ½-mile stretch of meadow, is for skiers of intermediate or better skills.

Drive Highway 97 to Swauk Pass, elevation 4102 feet, and the south-side Sno-Park. A Forest Service map board helps untangle the maze of trails and roads.

The Swauk Meadow Trail starts in conjunction with Haney Meadow Trail (Trail 57). At ¾ mile look both ways for roaring snowmobiles and

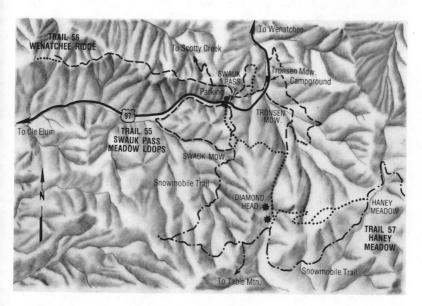

One of many twisted trees on the Campground Loops

dart across Table Mountain road. Ski through a short belt of forest and head uphill, parting company with the Haney Meadow route. Climb over a small knoll, recross the forest road, and enjoy a long run down Swauk Meadow. At the bottom bear right into a second meadow. Follow blue diamonds into woods for an exhilarating run down a skid road. The highway returns you to the Sno-Park.

Campground Loops. These 2½ miles of intermediate-level trails can be entered either from Swauk Pass at the north-side Sno-Park or from Tronsen Campground, 3600 feet, 1 mile down the highway on the north side of the pass.

Tronsen Campground is popular for snow play, and ski tours of up to ½ mile can be made around the campsites. The longer loops start opposite the section signed "Picnic Only." Head uphill to an open slope and climb to the top. Take a skid road to the right and follow it to within 100 feet of the end. Climb uphill through a small basin and then up a rounded knoll to twisted trees and views of the Stuart Range. Ski left, back to the skid road, to complete the loop. Or invent your own variations.

Tronsen Meadow. This is the least technically demanding of the loops, the 5 miles lying entirely on logging roads except for one short section of steep forest trail. Meadows offer plenty of room for snow play and numerous spur roads invite explorations. One hitch: The loop doesn't quite close and ½ mile of road must be walked between the trip start on Tronsen Meadow road and the end on Upper Tronsen road.

Park at Tronsen Campground, elevation 3600 feet, and walk .2 miles back up to Tronsen Meadow road. Ski up this road and follow blue diamonds on forest trail to the upper road. A short sidetrip leads to views across rolling hills to jagged peaks of the Stuart Range.

For a 9-mile superloop adventure, take the trail that links the Tronsen Meadow Loop to the Haney Meadow Trail, proceed over Swauk Meadow, then cross the highway to the Campground Loops and so back to the car.

SWAUK CREEK

56 WENATCHEE RIDGE

Skill level basic and up
Round trip to road-end 6 miles
Skiing time 4 hours
Elevation gain 458 feet
High point 4560 feet
Best January-February
Avalanche potential low
USGS Liberty

Map—page 141

Ridge after ridge of gleaming, snow-covered hills, capped by Mt. Adams, Mt. Rainier, and Mt. Stuart, are viewed from a top-of-the-world route along the crest of Wenatchee Ridge. If that isn't enough, the area has skiing for everyone from gung-ho 5-year-olds to their telemarking parents.

Drive Highway 97 to Swauk Pass, elevation 4102 feet, and park in the north-side Sno-Park. A large Forest Service information and map board helps travelers orient themselves in the maze of roads.

The road sets out east from the information board. Although most snowmobiles stay to the south side of the pass, expect to see a few on the

Stuart Range from the Wenatchee Ridge road

first ½ mile. In 150 feet the road swings left (north) and the way to the Swauk Pass Meadow Loops (Trail 55) branches right, marked with bright blue triangles. Follow the road as it winds above the pass, gaining 200 feet in the first ½ mile, to reach a small pass and junction. Scotty Creek road descends straight ahead into snowmobile country. Turn left on Wenatchee Ridge road.

Unlike other ski trails in the Swauk Pass area, the ridge road soon breaks out of forest and the whole world opens up on either side. The way rolls along, dropping from the ridge top to contour around the higher peaks, then returning to the crest. Small knolls are scenic lunch spots as well as fun ski hills. Advanced skiers will find clearcut slopes of various steepness to challenge their turning abilities.

Save some energy for the road-end clearcut. Just before 3 miles the road splits. Climb the upper fork to the top of a small knoll for a final overlook of Red Top Mountain, Swauk valley, and lowlands beyond.

It is possible to follow the ridge another 2 miles to Blewett Pass, but as of this writing there is no trail through the dense forest.

SWAUK CREEK

57 HANEY MEADOW

Skill level advanced
Round trip via trail route 10 miles
Skiing time 8 hours
Elevation gain 1860 feet
High point 5960 feet
Best January–February
Avalanche potential moderate
USGS Liberty

Map—page 141

Skiing fresh powder

Excellent snow and surprising views make the country around Haney Meadow a place for endless, happy hours on skis. The white meadow plain, ringed by forested hills, is a great basecamp for days of exploring logging roads, trails, and ridge crests.

Drive Highway 97 to Swauk Pass and park in the Sno-Park on the south side, elevation 4102 feet.

There are two ways to Haney Meadow. One is the Table Mountain road, which gets there in 9 comparatively gentle miles. It is easy to

Tronsen Ridge from the Haney Meadow Trail

follow except near the Table Mountain turnoff, where it sometimes is obscured by drifting snow; in that case continue to contour and watch for silver markers on trees. This route is worth considering when snow is icy or avalanche hazard high. However, snow pilots abound on weekends, snarling and roaring, hitting speeds of 40 to 50 miles per hour, and open roads and meadows seem to bring out their kamikaze instincts.

The wise and quiet choice is the steep, rugged, and well-marked skier-only trail that leads to the meadow in 5 miles. Haney Meadow Trail begins in conjunction with Swauk Meadow Loop (Trail 55). From the information board at the start of Table Mountain road bear right over the top of the snow-play clearing. At the west side turn uphill on an old skid road. The ski trail jaunts ¾ mile through timber to the Table Mountain road; poke your head out, look carefully both ways for hurtling machines, and scamper across.

Pass through a narrow strip of trees to a small clearing and the Haney junction at 1 mile, 4320 feet. For Haney Meadow take the left fork (straight ahead), which crosses the clearing and contours around Diamond Head. At 2½ miles, 4500 feet, Tronsen Meadow Trail joins from the north. The Haney Meadow trail now gets to serious work, climbing a narrow valley on the east side of Diamond Head and crossing two avalanche chutes. In times of avalanche potential, detour down into the trees.

The trail ascends around the valley head and up open slopes on the far side. A tall, lone tree near the top marks another intersection at 4 miles, 5840 feet. A 1-mile trail goes right to the Table Mountain razzers. The Haney Meadow Trail continues straight ahead to the forest edge, then turns right to climb up and down a knoll.

At 4½ miles, 5960 feet, the trail splits. Both forks lead to the meadows; the left is best for views. A short climb attains a ridge with a broad panorama of the Cascades, featuring the Stuart Range; this is the proper destination-turnaround for day-tourers. The right fork traverses around the ridge to rejoin the left and the united way drops ½ mile to the end of an old spur road which leads down 100 feet to the Table Mountain road. Turn right for the final short drop to Haney Meadow, 5502 feet.

Are you camping? Include these in your day trips: Mt. Lillian, Upper Naneum Meadows, Mission Ridge Ski Area via road No. 2107, and Lion Rock via road No. 2008, long but very scenic.

Grand Park and Mt. Rainier from Scarface

58 GRAND PARK

Skill level advanced
Round trip 25 miles
Skiing time 2-3 days
Elevation gain 3540 feet
High point 5640 feet
Best January-March
Avalanche potential low
USGS Greenwater and Sunrise

Map—page 147

With the exception of Paradise, most of Mt. Rainier National Park in winter is strictly for major expeditions. However, a backdoor entry lets skiers who have 2 to 3 days at their disposal attain the wide meadow terrace of Grand Park, just a stone's throw from the northeast base of "The Mountain." Unfortunately, the access road may be cluttered on weekends by machinery.

Drive Highway 410 east from Enumclaw 24.2 miles and turn right on Huckleberry Creek road No. 73. In midwinter (and in this description) the skiing starts here, elevation 2100 feet. Park well off the road, leaving plenty of room for others.

A few hundred yards from the highway is a Y; turn left and follow road No. 73 for 9½ miles. Many spurs lead to excellent day-skiing, but for the long, high trip stay on the valley floor, winding along Huckleberry Creek, crossing it at 6 miles, 2960 feet. From the crossing the road gains elevation quickly for 1½ miles and then, at 3680 feet, bends sharply into Eleanor Creek drainage. The grade now gentles. In another 2 miles the road sharply bends to cross Eleanor Creek, 4480 feet. Leave the road—and the snow machines—and enter forest left (east) of Eleanor Creek. In a few yards is the park boundary, a perfect spot for a basecamp in the protection of the trees and the National Park.

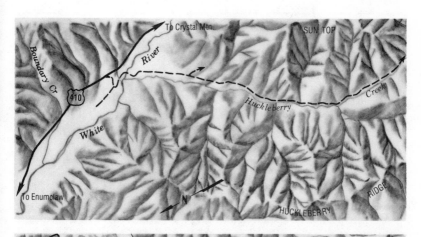

The next 3 miles are an unmarked route through the trees to Grand Park. From the National Park boundary head south-southwest, keeping to the left of the small valley between Scarface to the west and the ridge to the east. If you come to Lake Eleanor, you have gone too far right (west). Contour south around the base of Scarface and head up the next valley.

The route gradually gains elevation until ¼ mile before entering Grand Park. Here a quick 200 feet are climbed to the flat meadowland with broad views of the Carbon, Winthrop, and Emmons glaciers. If your eyes weary of all that great heap of snow, look away—to lower peaks, to snow-hung trees, to critter tracks on the white plain.

WHITE RIVER

59 BULLION BASIN

Skill level mountaineer
Round trip 4 miles
Skiing time 5 hours
Elevation gain 1800 feet
High point 5900 feet
Best mid-December–May
Avalanche potential moderate
USGS Bumping Lake

Map—page 151

Bullion Basin is a perfect example of the challenging to extremely difficult skiing to be found in Silver Creek drainage. The mountains seem to rise straight out of the valley floor and the basin is the merest niche cut into rugged talus. Sheltered in its shady nooks and crannies, however, the snow remains light and powdery long after snow elsewhere has turned to corn or melted. The approach to this hidden winter wonderland is not easy, starting with a climb of 800 feet up narrow and icy downhill tracks—even trickier to descend on the return. Luckily, most weekdays this hill is not used.

Drive Highway 410 east from Enumclaw to the gated entrance to Mt. Rainier National Park. Turn left and drive to the end of the Crystal Mountain road and the downhill parking area, elevation 4200 feet. Register with the ski patrol and get the latest update on avalanche conditions.

Bullion Basin is located above Chair 7. Skiers choosing not to ride the lift will find the Blue Bell Run, starting just to the right of the chair, one of the least strenuous of the many difficult ways up. Climb to the chair's uppermost terminal, 5130 feet.

Two routes lead to the basin. On the left side of the valley a steep jeep

Skier on the Bullion Basin Trail

road cuts an obvious path, but this area is extremely avalanche-prone and should be avoided. Stay to the right instead, climbing to the top of a sparsely timbered knob behind the chair. Keep right along the valley wall on level terrain and then, as the slope steepens, enter dense timber. At 5500 feet cross the first of several small clearings. Bullion Basin lies only 200 feet above. In the last ¼ mile climb through sparse forest to either side of the prominent center knob.

For further skiing head right, climbing a thinly timbered rib to the ridge crest. Turn right (south) along the ridge to its end at Crown Point, 6490 feet. An overnight trip can be made to Norse Peak by going north along the ridge.

60 SILVER BASIN

SILVER BASIN

Skill level advanced
Round trip 4½ miles from parking lot
Skiing time 4 hours
Elevation gain 1800 feet
High point 6000 feet
Best mid-December–May
Avalanche potential low
USGS Bumping Lake

BEAR GAP

Skill level advanced
Round trip 4½ miles
Skiing time 4 hours
Elevation gain 1682 feet
High point 5882 feet
Best mid-December–March
Avalanche potential low
USGS Bumping Lake

Map—page 151

Completely hidden from the noise and hard-packed slopes of the Crystal Mountain Ski Area, Silver Basin lies secluded by steep mountain walls in a fairy-tale world of winter beauty. Deep, fluffy powder often covers the small lakes, open meadows, and hillsides, offering a variety of skiing from serene gliding to mad downhill thrills. Bear Gap gives untracked snow and views to corniced ridges and snowbound Cascade Mountains.

Silver Basin

Park at Crystal Mountain Ski Area parking lot (Trail 59), elevation 4200 feet. Be sure to register with the Ski Patrol and check on avalanche conditions before starting out.

Silver Basin. The first 1000 feet to Silver Basin can be gained by skiing up the Quicksilver Run (climbing skins will help) or riding Chair 4. From the chair top, 5420 feet, a snow cat often sets a track to Silver Basin. If no track can be seen, head southwest towards Hen Skin Lake, reached in ½ mile. Circle the east shore and proceed west, continually gaining elevation. Another long ¼ mile passes two more small, snow-covered lakes to an open meadow, 5580 feet. Follow this long clearing southwest into Silver Basin. The wide-open slopes above are prime cross-country downhilling terrain. If snow conditions are stable, ski up to the ridge for a breathtaking view of Mt. Rainier.

The return retraces the route to the top of Chair 4, then takes one of the downhill runs to the bottom. The Tinkerbell Run to the left (west) of Quicksilver is suggested since it usually is the least mogulled. Amaze the wobbly beginners on downhill skis with your grace and control on the long skinny boards.

Bear Gap. From the parking lot ski up the Boondoggle Run or ride Chair 4 and ski to the southeast end of Boondoggle, 5460 feet. Head southeast in untracked snow, aiming for the lowest saddle in the ridge, Bear Gap, 5882 feet, a long ¾ mile from the top of Chair 4. Cross the gap to views south and east, the perfect lunch spot on a sunny day. The return to Chair 4 is a long, rolling downhill run.

Mt. Rainier from a shoulder of Naches Peak

WHITE RIVER

61 CHINOOK PASS AND NACHES PEAK (false summit)

CHINOOK PASS

Skill level intermediate and up
Round trip 4 miles
Skiing time 2 hours
Elevation gain 832 feet
High point 5432 feet
Best November and December
Avalanche potential low
USGS Chinook Pass

NACHES PEAK (false summit)

Skill level advanced
Round trip 7 miles
Skiing time 4 hours
Elevation gain 1760 feet
High point 6360 feet
Best November and December
Avalanche potential moderate
USGS Chinook Pass

Map—page 153

Skiing in the Chinook Pass–Naches Peak area starts with the first major snowstorms to hit the Cascades. There is great fun to be had challenging the open bowls leading to Dewey Lakes or simply taking in incomparable views of Mt. Rainier.

The skiing season around Chinook Pass starts and ends early. Beginning as soon as Highway 410 is closed over the pass, it ends when 4694-foot Cayuse Pass is snowed in, usually by mid- to late-December. In late spring there is often another week or two of skiing before the snowplows come to end the fun.

No entry up closed Highway 410 is recommended during mid-winter. There are several steep avalanche slide areas along the roadway, making travel extremely hazardous.

Chinook Pass. From Enumclaw drive Highway 410 for 41 miles to the summit of Cayuse Pass and park. Do not, under any circumstances, walk or ski the road as it is extremely prone to avalanches.

On skis, contour through the trees below the Chinook Pass Highway heading southeast for ¼ to ½ mile, before heading uphill. Be sure to stay well away from the highway and in the protection of the trees. After ½ mile of climbing steeply, the forest route bisects the highway where it makes a sharp switchback north. Follow the creek or the road to reach 5294-foot Tipsoo Lake and excellent views of Mt. Rainier from the snowbound bowl. The road can be followed for the final ½ mile to Chinook Pass. Skiing beyond the pass is not recommended as the steep slopes are avalanche prone.

Naches Peak (the false summit). From Tipsoo Lake, follow the road another 500 feet and climb to the smaller Tipsoo Lake. Then ski south up a lightly timbered ridge. When the open slope below a ridge running west from the false summit of Naches Peak is reached, traverse west in order to gain the ridge, avoiding the cornices above. Once on the ridge crest, follow its south side to the false summit of Naches Peak, the 6360-foot chief viewpoint of the trip. From the false summit, ski out to Dewey Lakes or just be satisfied with a great run back to the car. Sections of the descent are steep so be sure your turns and stopping ability are in good form.

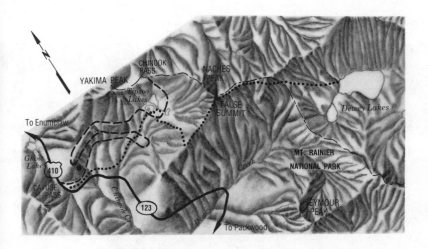

62 PLEASANT VALLEY LOOP

Skill level basic and up
Round trip to Pleasant Valley Campground 6 miles
Skiing time 4 hours
Elevation gain 400 feet
High point 3600 feet
Best January–mid-April
Avalanche potential none
USGS Bumping Lake

Map—page 155

Sandwiched between steep walls of the Fifes Peaks and American Ridge, Pleasant Valley melts out slower than surrounding ridges. The Forest Service has developed a 6-mile cross-country loop that allows skiers to take advantage of the lingering snow while skimming along a tree-lined trail. The two legs of the loop, on opposite sides of American River, differ radically. The southeast leg follows a narrow trail along a rolling hillside, suitable for intermediate skiers or better. The northwest side follows a skid road which is wide, open, and nearly level the whole distance—good skiing for everyone.

The loop lies between Hells Crossing Campground and Pleasant Valley Campground. There is parking at each place. Up river from Pleasant Valley Campground are 2 more miles of trail that the Forest Service hopes to include in a new loop in the near future.

From the intersection of Highways 410 and 12, drive 33.3 miles

Bridge over the American River at Pleasant Valley Campground

Bear tracks in spring snow

towards Chinook Pass on 410 to Hells Crossing Campground and park in the small turnout provided, elevation 3280 feet. The alternate start is at Pleasant Valley Campground, 3.3 miles farther. Be sure to carry chains and shovel at all times on this road; it is plowed on a low-priority basis, once a week at most.

To do the full loop from Hells Crossing Campground, begin with the southeast leg, climbing above the American River. Starting just before the highway bridge, the trail ascends in sight and sound of the rushing river, then enters a forest world stilled in winter except for an occasional breeze or the call of a lonely bird impatient for spring. The ascent yields to a rollercoaster path through tall pines. Occasional windows in the

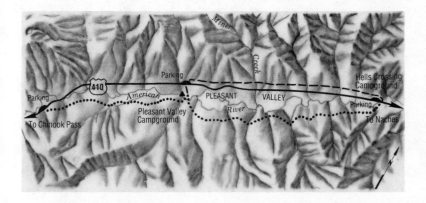

forest open out on the rugged Fifes Peaks to the north. At 3 miles descend back to the river. At 100 feet before the bridge a trail branches left up the valley, in 2 more scenic miles meeting Highway 410.

The loop trail crosses the American River, passes through Pleasant Valley Campground, and crosses the highway, 3440 feet. A short climb through trees reaches the skid road, an easy slide back down the valley. This leg has no scenic viewpoints but plenty to see; compare nature's handiwork to man's as the road passes from virgin forest to selectively logged areas. The loop is closed at 5 miles. Ski through Hells Crossing Campground and thence to the starting point.

NACHES RIVER

63 ROCKY PRAIRIE

Skill level intermediate and up
Round trip 4-18 miles
Skiing time 3 hours-2 days
Elevation gain 600-1617 feet
High point 5898 feet
Best December-April
Avalanche potential low
USGS Nile and Manastash Lake

Map—page 157

Skiing starts in late fall and lasts late into spring on the broad, rolling ridges high above the Naches River. Miles of open prairies invite explor-

Rocky Prairie

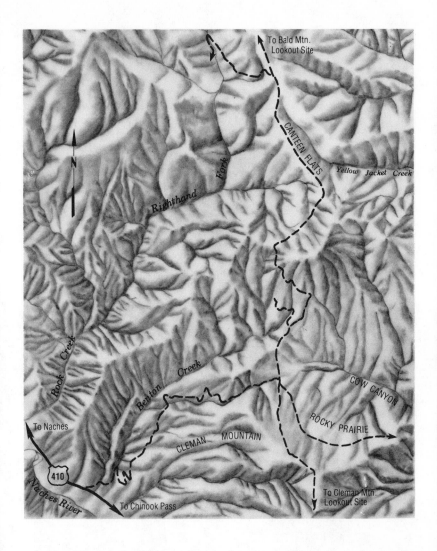

ation, and roads lead to overlooks of innumerable peaks in the South Cascades.

Drive Highway 410 west from the Highway 12 junction for 13.4 miles. Turn right on Benton Creek road No. 1732 (old number system), elevation 2160 feet. Drive to the snowline and park.

Winter trippers start at or close to the valley bottom, with 4 miles of road to ski to reach the highlands. This is snowmobile country and skiers are the oddity, so expect a few of the bolder machines to come sniffing around trying to figure out what those creatures are that move without gas tanks.

The climb starts immediately. Follow the road as it sweeps up above the Naches River with excellent views of houses and fields below. At 1½ miles stay left at a major intersection with road No. 1605. The final 2½ miles to the ridge crest are in forest.

An open plain and a four-way intersection mark the arrival at Rocky Prairie, 3787 feet, a good basecamp for exploration. Skiers may go right 7 miles to Cleman Mountain Lookout, 5115 feet, or left (north) 8 miles to Bald Mountain Lookout, 5898 feet. For a little less far-flung trip, ski right ¼ mile towards Cleman Mountain, then go left 2 miles on the Rocky Prairie road, with views to rolling hills and shimmering plains of Washington's Inland Empire.

Early and late in the season, skiers may drive all the way to Rocky Prairie, then take a left for Bald Mountain. The road climbs over a large hill to level off on Canteen Flats, 4288 feet. If there is no snow here, continue north over another hill to a set of flats below Bald Mountain at 5000 feet or ski to the old Bald Mountain Lookout.

Best of all, leave roads altogether and roam for miles towards whatever tree, hill, or horizon seems intriguing.

Cross-country skiing is a sport enjoyed at any age

64 MOWICH LAKE

Skill level basic and up
Round trip 11 miles
Skiing time 6 hours
Elevation gain 1410 feet
High point 4960 feet
Best March–April
Avalanche potential low
USGS Gold Lakes and Mowich Lake

Map—page 159

Nestled in the forest at the base of glacier-wrapped Mt. Rainier, Mowich Lake is an excellent tour for a day or weekend outing. While the area has prime skiing throughout the winter, access problems make this trip best in spring when the roads are snowfree at least to the park boundary.

Drive Highway 410 to Buckley. From the west end of town turn south on Highway 165 for 10.5 miles, passing through Wilkeson and crossing the Fairfax bridge over the Carbon River. At the junction beyond take the right fork to Mowich Lake. A "Road Closed" sign here indicates the road receives no winter plowing or maintenance. The pavement ends at 1.3 miles; 10 more miles on a dirt road lead to the boundary of Mt. Rainier National Park, elevation 3550 feet, and the start of the tour.

There are two ways to ski to the lake, 5½ miles on the road or by a 4½-mile road-and-trail combination suited for skiers with advanced-level or better skills. The two routes begin together on the Mowich Lake road.

Ski through dense forest, passing the Pauls Peak picnic area ¾ mile

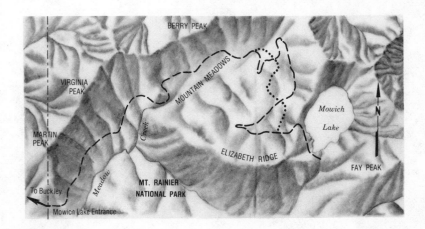

from the park boundary. The road climbs gently but steadily above Meadow Creek to the end of the valley. At 3 miles, 4280 feet, it makes a long curve to the south, starting the long, winding climb to the lake. Here the trail's first section leaves the road to ascend a shallow gully ¼ mile to a crossing of the road. The second section of trail stays just left of a small creek ½ mile, intersecting the road again at 4640 feet. The third and final ½-mile section of trail is the steepest, rejoining the road at 4920 feet. Once back on the road (if you ever got off it), turn left and ski to its high point on the west side of Mowich Lake, 4960 feet. If in doubt about the trail, stay on the road. (The Park Service may start marking the trail in years to come.)

Campsites are found at the road-end on the south side of the lake and viewpoints on the west side. For vistas from the high point of the road, ski left up a forested ridge until Mt. Rainier comes in sight over the lake. Watch the thundering spring avalanches cascade down the sheer rock face of Willis Wall.

Mt. Rainier from Mowich Lake road

65 REFLECTION LAKES

Skill level intermediate and up
Round trip to Reflection Lakes 3 miles
Skiing time 2 hours
Elevation gain 538 feet
High point 5100 feet
Best January–mid-April
Avalanche potential low
USGS Mt. Rainier East

Map—page 163

Reflection Lake and Mt. Rainier

In summer the Reflection Lakes reflect flowers of surrounding meadows and glaciers of Mt. Rainier. Most visitors pause briefly to click cameras and drive on. In winter, however, though the little snow-covered lakes reflect nothing but the sun, they are the objective of numerous day trips and overnight outings.

From the Nisqually Entrance to Mt. Rainier National Park follow the Paradise road to Narada Falls viewpoint, elevation 4572 feet. In winter a large parking area is plowed for skiers and the warming hut–restroom facility is kept open.

From the parking lot the aim is to gain Stevens Canyon road on the top of the steep hill straight ahead. Skiers often climb directly up the open slope behind the warming hut, but avalanche hazard rules out this approach. The safe way is to start near the warming hut and stay in the forest, climbing the left side of the open slope. The farther to the left, the easier the grade.

Once on the Stevens Canyon road, if the snow is stable, follow the road across the windswept hillside above the warming hut and another mile of easy going to the lakes. The hillside should never be skied when conditions are unstable. If in doubt, ask a ranger before starting. If there is a possibility of avalanches, ski to the old Paradise valley road, follow it a short way and pick up a ski trail, marked with orange poles, that climbs over the top of Mazama Ridge, 5100 feet, then descends to the Stevens Canyon road. Ski the road ¼ mile left to the largest Reflection Lake, 4861 feet.

At the lake, an obvious option is to wander the snowy meadows. Another is to visit Louise Lake. To do so, continue on the road a mile and as it begins a sharp bend to the head of Stevens Canyon leave it on the left and descend due west to the lake, 4592 feet.

Other popular tours are the Tatoosh Range (Trail 66) and to Paradise via Mazama Ridge (Trail 67).

The Castle, left, and Pinnacle Peak, right, from Reflection Lakes

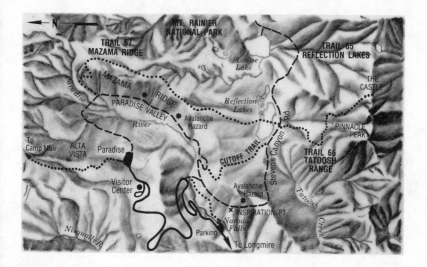

66 TATOOSH RANGE

Skill level advanced
Round trip 5 miles
Skiing time 4 hours
Elevation gain 1432 feet
High point 6000 feet
Best January–April
Avalanche potential moderate
USGS Mt. Rainier East

Map—page 163

As viewed from a small saddle on the side of Castle Peak in the Tatoosh Range, the enormous bulk of Mt. Rainier fills the entire northern horizon. Below lies a basin whose deep snow generally is much drier than that across the valley at Paradise. To the east a long ridge and open slopes stretch more than a mile towards Unicorn Peak.

From the Nisqually Entrance to Mt. Rainier National Park drive to the Narada Falls viewpoint parking area, elevation 4572 feet. Ski to Reflection Lakes (see Trail 65), 4854 feet.

Skiers who have hiked this area in the summer are familiar with the two trails from the Reflection Lakes vicinity up into the Tatoosh Range, the Bench and Snow Lakes Trail and the Pinnacle Saddle Trail. Both are highly avalanche-prone in winter. There is, however, a relatively avalanche-free entry to the Tatoosh Range via Castle Saddle.

Ski the Stevens Canyon road halfway around Reflection Lakes. At a

Mt. Rainier from Castle Basin

convenient point leave the road and start uphill into a big basin with a steep headwall. The avalanche-free route climbs the right side of the basin in the fringe of trees atop a rib. Still in trees, cross the top of the headwall and climb into another big basin between Pinnacle Peak on the right and Castle on the left. Follow the treeline on the left of the basin. When the trees end, climb the last 200 feet of steep open slopes on the east side of Castle to the crest of the Tatoosh Range, 6000 feet.

Look south to the three southern giants—the dark, steaming mass of Mt. St. Helens, the sharp peak of Mt. Hood, and the rounded mass of Mt. Adams. All three are dwarfed by massive Mt. Rainier to the north.

For most skiers the saddle is enough. However, those who wish to go farther (when the snow is stable) can cross to the south side of the saddle and head east to the next small hill, staying well away from the corniced summit. Continue to a saddle, 6000 feet, below Unicorn Glacier. This is a good turnaround; beyond, the avalanche potential is high.

67 MAZAMA RIDGE

Skill level advanced
Round trip 6 miles
Skiing time 4 hours
Elevation gain 900 feet in, 900 feet out
High point 5700 feet
Best January–mid-May
Avalanche potential moderate
USGS Mt. Rainier East

Map—page 163

Ski snowy meadows of Mazama Ridge between the ancient Tatoosh Range and the young giant of the Cascades, Mt. Rainier.

The traditional Mazama tour starts at Paradise, follows the ridge crest down to Reflection Lakes, then returns via the Paradise valley road. Several areas on this trip are prone to avalanches. One, just east of In-

Skiing the open meadows of Mazama Ridge

spiration Point, may be avoided by the Reflection Lakes Cutoff Trail. The second, in the middle section of the Paradise valley road, can be missed by skiing in the center of the valley. When conditions are unstable, however, the safest policy is to go somewhere else; if in doubt, ask a ranger before setting out.

From the upper Paradise parking lot, elevation 5450 feet, follow the Paradise valley road below Paradise Inn. Descend gently past the second snow-covered bridge, 5200 feet, then immediately turn left and head uphill. The climb starts steep but levels out on a small bench. Ski to the upper end of the bench and climb right on open slopes to Mazama Ridge, 5700 feet.

Explore the rolling ridge crest, uninhibited by summer signs that tell you to "Stay on the Trail" and "Keep off the Meadows." Ski on a rolling cushion of snow north towards Panorama Point or to the open basin below the Paradise Glacier a little to the east.

Heading down Mazama Ridge, stay to the right along the ridge top. Near the end of the ridge, the broad plateau falls away. Ski just east of the ridge crest, angling right to several green south-facing slopes, then head down through timber. Near the bottom, bear right to reach Reflection Lakes at 2½ miles, 4861 feet.

The return may be made either on the same route or up the road. If the road is chosen, ski to the south side of Reflection Lakes and take a right on Stevens Canyon road. About ¼ mile past the lakes go uphill along the summer trail, marked with orange stakes. Cross Mazama Ridge on the Cutoff Trail and descend the other side steeply to Paradise valley road. A left turn leads to the Narada Falls parking area. A right turn leads up the Paradise valley road to the starting point.

The Castle and Pinnacle Peak from Mazama Ridge

Horizontal ice crystals show the fury of a winter storm at Camp Muir

---

MT. RAINIER

68 CAMP MUIR

GLACIER VISTA

Skill level intermediate and up
Round trip 3 miles
Skiing time 2 hours
Elevation gain 1022 feet
High point 6336 feet
Best December–April
Avalanche potential low
USGS Mt. Rainier East

Map—pages 163 and 169

CAMP MUIR

Skill level mountaineer
Round trip 9 miles
Skiing time 8 hours
Elevation gain 4500 feet
High point 10,000 feet
Best mid-October–mid-July
Avalanche potential moderate
USGS Mt. Rainier East

Though the snow is best from mid-October to mid-July, diehards ski the year around at one place or another between Paradise and Camp Muir. Winter skiers generally are satisfied with the steep slopes at Glacier Vista below Panorama Point. Those continuing to Camp Muir should be proficient mountaineers ready to deal with sudden whiteouts and blasting winds. In summer the snowline retreats to the base of the perma-

nent icefield above Pebble Creek, elevation 7500 feet. Even in these milder months be prepared for sudden changes of weather and fogs that erase all landmarks.

Note: When snow conditions are unstable or an east wind is blowing, causing a slab avalanche to form, Panorama Point has high avalanche potential. Stay away after a heavy snowfall, when the wind blows from the east, or during winter rains.

The tour starts from the upper Paradise parking lot, elevation 5450 feet. At the start and finish of the trip register in the log book at the ranger's office.

Ski to the left of Alta Vista, then up snowy meadows past forlorn clumps of windblown trees to Glacier Vista at 1½ miles, 6336 feet. This overlook of the Nisqually Glacier is an ideal picnic spot and turnaround for winter skiers.

To proceed to Camp Muir in summer, when the snow has melted, follow the well-marked trail up the steep west face of Panorama Point. When there is snow, however, avoid the trail and climb through a broken line of dwarf trees to the right of the face on the southwest corner of the Point. Skis generally are removed in favor of postholing.

Head over the rolling summit of Panorama Point, up and to the right. Ski along the left side of the prominent rock outcrops of McClure Rock and Sugar Loaf, aiming for the next knob, Anvil Rock.

Skirt it on the left and ascend the last long snowfield to Camp Muir, 10,000 feet.

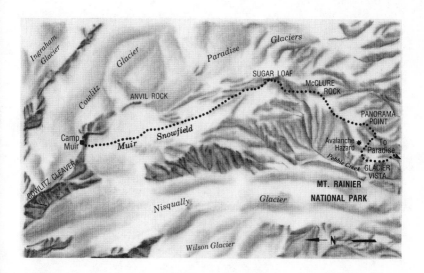

Midsummer tour to Camp Muir

69 BURLEY MOUNTAIN

Skill level intermediate and up
Round trip up to 18 miles to lookout
Skiing time up to 2 days
Elevation gain 3931 feet
High point 5304 feet
Best November–December and March–April
Avalanche potential low
USGS Greenhorn Buttes and Tower Rock

Map—page 170

From the valley Burley Mountain seems to be just one of many ridges bristling with dense second-growth forest. Those who make the long climb to the top, however, find that the miles of unrelieved timber lead to sparkling snow-covered meadows and a lookout with views which include the three southern volcanoes of Washington.

The first 7 miles of the Burley Mountain road are wooded and viewless. Most skiers therefore do the trip when it is drivable the first couple of miles. In May they are advised to check first with the Randle Ranger Station because the road is gated in late spring to protect the winter-softened grade while it dries out.

Drive to Randle. Just east of the grocery store turn off Highway 12 on the Mt. Adams–Cispus Center road heading south. When the road splits at .9 mile, stay left on the Cispus road, which becomes road No. 23. At 8.3 miles go right on road No. 28 for 1.4 miles, then take another right on

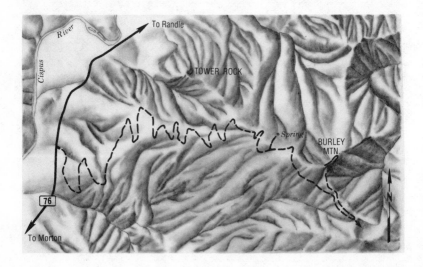

Snow doughnuts fresh off the slope

road No. 76. Drive 2.2 miles, passing the Cispus Center and the small community of Tower Rock, where the pavement ends, to reach Burley Mountain road No. 7605. Park at the junction, elevation 1273 feet, or at the snowline.

The Burley Mountain road starts right off climbing. Switchbacks through dense forest cover reach the first meadow at 6 miles, 4260 feet, a good campsite. A short spur branches left 1000 feet to a spring (do not expect running water in winter).

The big meadows start at 7 miles as the road emerges on open slopes beneath the lookout. If snow conditions are unstable, this is the proper turnaround.

The final section of road climbs to meet a long ridge south of the lookout. The road continues 4.5 miles to Poal Patch Campground; however, Burley Mountain skiers take the left branch back to the plainly visible lookout—or climb the open meadows and cut off nearly 2 miles of road-skiing.

Once at the lookout let the eye wander southwest towards the steaming remains of the once-mighty Mt. St. Helens, then farther east to the still-mighty Mt. Adams, and finally north to the mightiest of all, Mt. Rainier.

70 PACKWOOD LAKE

Skill level advanced
Round trip from parking lot 9 miles
Skiing time 7 hours
Elevation gain 500 feet
High point 3200 feet
Best January–April
Avalanche potential low
USGS Packwood

Map—page 173

Spring skiing

An example of the difference a blanket of snow can make: Packwood Lake in summer is a turmoil of loud motorcycles and mobs trampling shores on the edge of the Goat Rocks Wilderness. In winter it is a silent island of pristine white in a sea of green peace. In summer a 4½-mile trail leads to the lake. In midwinter, if the weather so decides, there may be up to 6 additional miles of road-skiing, and a party may then be well content with the trailhead parking lot's view over the Cowlitz River valley to the Tatoosh Range and Mt. Rainier. If the lake is the inflexible goal, skiers had best wait until late March or April, when the road is snowfree to the end.

Note: Snowmobilers and skiers used to bypass the trail by following the Pipeline road to the dam. Slides now have closed this road to all forms of winter travel.

Drive Highway 12 to Packwood Ranger Station, 1100 feet, and then 6 miles (if snow allows) on Packwood Lake road to the end, elevation 2700 feet.

Starting at the east end of the parking lot, the trail is wide, well graded, and easy to follow over gentle ups and downs. At 3½ miles a window in virgin forest looks north to Rainier. The steepest travel is the final ½ mile, where the trail drops 200 feet to the lake and campsites, 2900 feet.

From here the horizon is domineered by huge walls of 7487-foot Johnson Peak. For a change of scenery ski Upper Lake Creek Trail along the east shore, to where Packwood Lake and enclosing forests form a perfect frame for the jolly white giant of the Cascades, Mt. Rainier.

Packwood Lake Trail

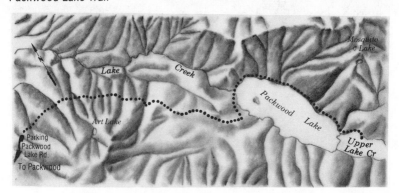

71 YELLOW JACKET ROAD

Skill level basic and up
Round trip to road-end 7 miles
Skiing time 4 hours
Elevation gain 480 feet
High point 4800 feet
Best January–mid-April
Avalanche potential low
USGS White Pass

Map—page 174

There is fun for all in the Yellow Jacket area. The road, nearly level, pleases beginners. Clearcuts challenge intermediates and advanced skiers in search of the perfect telemark. For everyone there are maximum views for a minimum climb, especially suited to skiers seeking the best in mountain scenery but not really wanting to tackle lofty summits on skinny skis.

Drive Highway 12 to .7 mile west of White Pass and turn north .1 mile to Yellow Jacket road No. 1284. Park well off to the side to allow road-maintenance equipment free access to the work center at the road-end, elevation 4320 feet.

Yellow Jacket road is a designated cross-country ski area, and consequently only a moderate number of snowmobiles get "lost" and end up here. One can follow the tracks of these poor lost souls as they wander around and around in circles.

Elevation is gained gradually along the tree-lined route. At ½ mile is

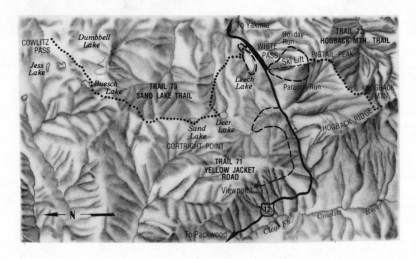

Trees in winter overcoats

the first clearcut, the best one for showing off downhill skills in linking turns. The road turns south across open slopes. Southeast, the upper lifts of the White Pass Ski Area come in view. Across the valley massive Hogback Ridge dominates the horizon. The road soon turns west and the Cowlitz River valley unfolds, a new segment being added with each clearcut traversed. On the horizon there at first is just Chimney Rock, but ultimately views extend deep into the Goat Rocks, all the way to 7930-foot Old Snowy Mountain. To the north the Tatoosh Range comes in view.

The climax of the trip is at the road-end at 3½ miles, 4800 feet. When the last corner is rounded Mt. Rainier emerges in full view, high and mighty above other peaks. Take a long lunch break before heading back to enjoy the miles of vistas.

The slopes of Hogback Mountain are excellent for telemarking

Hogback Mountain, right, from Pigtail Peak

72 HOGBACK MOUNTAIN

Skill level advanced
Round trip 5 miles
Skiing time 4 hours
Elevation gain 2309 feet
High point 6789 feet
Best December–mid-April
Avalanche potential low
USGS White Pass

Map—page 174

Rolling hills and delightful bowls lead to a grand panoramic overlook which encompasses miles of snow-topped peaks, featuring the impressive Goat Rocks and the giant of ice, Mt. Rainier.

Drive Highway 12 to White Pass and park in the White Pass Ski Area parking lot, elevation 4500 feet. Sign out at the ticket booth before heading into the backcountry.

A major portion of the climb can be avoided by taking the chairlift (Chair 1 or 2) to the top of Pigtail Peak. Skiers with more energy or less money—or purer hearts—may wish to ski all the way up. To do so follow the edge of the Holiday Run or, for the most direct route, the Paradise Run, located on the far right of the ski area. To make the Ski Patrol happy, start up before 8 a.m. to avoid the downhill rush. Aim for a saddle 200 feet below and south of the terminals.

If you ride to the top of Chair 1 or 2, 5961 feet, descend to the right (southwest) to meet the Holiday Run. Continue straight and drop to a lightly forested saddle a few hundred yards beyond the run; those who chose to ski up will be waiting for you here. Leaving the packed slopes for the freedom of the unpacked hills, ski across an open saddle, then head right along the broad ridge, staying close to the top.

Dodging trees is a full-time occupation for the first mile. The second mile leaves forest for open, subalpine terrain. Large bowls with moderate to steep slopes invite skiers to try their luck at a straight swoosh or a graceful telemark.

As Hogback Mountain draws near, a large rock knob is seen. Keep this landmark on the left and head up the final ridge to the summit of the peak, 6789 feet.

Open slopes beckon the skier towards the Goat Rocks, but the avalanche potential is so great that one does better to look, not ski. Instead explore the gentler terrain of Hogback's north ridge.

On the way home from the summit keep an eye on the chairlifts that crown Pigtail Peak. Return to forest below Pigtail and traverse to the right, picking up the Paradise Run. Tighten your belt, grit your teeth, rub your good luck charm, and then ski the downhill run back to the lodge. Please do not forget to sign out.

COWLITZ RIVER

73 SAND LAKE

SAND LAKE

Skill level intermediate and up
Round trip to Sand Lake 7 miles
Skiing time 6 hours
Elevation gain 895 feet
High point 5295 feet
Best January–mid-May
Avalanche potential none
USGS White Pass

COWLITZ PASS

Skill level advanced
Round trip to pass 16 miles
Skiing time 2–3 days
Elevation gain 1200 feet in, 500 feet out
High point 5600 feet
Best January–May
Avalanche potential low
USGS White Pass

Map—page 174

Ski to one subalpine lake or to a hundred. Climb to the top of one or many of the countless hills for the sheer pleasure of coming down, or save energy and dignity by contouring. No matter what kind of cross-country is your cup of tea, the Pacific Crest Trail north of White Pass probably has it. Skiers with only one day may travel to Deer and Sand lakes. Those with two or more days can continue to the center of the lakes area at Cowlitz Pass, a wonderful basecamp for explorations.

Drive Highway 12 east of White Pass summit .5 mile and park at the far end of the downhill ski area parking lot, elevation 4400 feet. Ski through a narrow band of trees to a prepared cross-country track around Leech Lake. Turn right on the track to the northeast end of the lake and the Pacific Crest Trail.

The trail starts off in forest, switchbacking up a small knoll; the way is usually well tracked and easy to follow as far as Deer Lake. After a new snowfall, however, someone has to be first and it may be you, so be sure to carry a map and compass to navigate over the forested ridges. A brief description: After leaving Leech Lake, when nearing the top of the first hill, head left over a shallow saddle, then contour left around the backside of the open hill above Leech Lake. At 2 miles pass a large meadow on the right. Continue climbing to the left (west) up a steep ridge. A short descent down the opposite side leads to Deer Lake, 5206 feet.

Beyond Deer Lake the trail turns north (right). Head along a broad ridge crest of open forest interspersed with pocket-size meadows. Sand Lake, 5295 feet, lies ½ mile beyond Deer Lake and is much more difficult to spot—its odd shape makes it look more like a meadow than a body of frozen water. Day skiers should turn around at Sand Lake or whenever they've had enough exploring.

The route beyond is a steady climb along the east side of the ridge in

The Pacific Crest Trail, south of Sand Lake

Deer Lake

view of Spiral Butte (an infant volcano) with occasional looks south to the Goat Rocks and Mt. Adams. At 5 miles, 5600 feet, the trail bends right to contour the east side of a partially forested hill, starting a descent that ends 1 mile later at Buesch Lake, 5080 feet. The trail skirts the right side of the lake, then climbs northeast to Cowlitz Pass, 5200 feet, to camping.

Numerous tours can be made from a basecamp here. Advanced skiers enjoy the ascent of 6340-foot Tumac Mountain (another potential St. Helens) to excellent views. Intermediate skiers find plenty of room for exploration among the lakes or in Blankenship Meadows on the north side of Tumac.

Continuing north on the Pacific Crest Trail from the lakes looks inviting on the map, but avalanche potential increases dramatically.

74 GOOSE EGG TRAIL

Skill level basic and up
Round trip 4 miles
Skiing time 3 hours
Elevation gain 50 feet
High point 2600 feet
Best January–March
Avalanche potential none
USGS Tieton Basin

Map—page 181

Tour a combination of trail and logging road along snow-covered banks of the Tieton River, sliding over small meadows in open pine forest.

Drive Highway 12 east from White Pass, 16.4 miles past Rimrock Lake to .6 mile west of Hause Creek Campground. Turn south on Tieton road and drive .2 mile to a large parking area on the right. A Forest Service information board marks the start of the trail, elevation 2550 feet.

Follow blue diamonds along the Tieton River, whose babbling drowns out noise of the busy highway and lets skiers enjoy the sound of their boards skimming the snow. The terrain is level except for the steep descent of a narrow path at 1 mile, immediately after the second crossing of a snowbound logging road. Skiers wishing to avoid the short drop may follow the phone lines to the left. The valley narrows as steep, rounded flanks of 4566-foot Goose Egg Mountain slope nearly to the river's edge. Ahead to the west is another dome looking even more like an egg. At 2 miles the trail ends by circling a small elbow of the river.

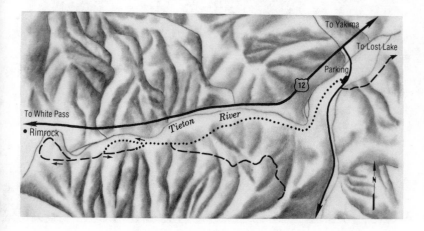

Across the water is the hamlet of Rimrock. A short bit upstream looms Rimrock Dam, holding back the 7-mile-long reservoir.

On the return, if time allows, take a sidetrip past a small lake for views north to imposing cliffs of Bethel Ridge. At mile 1, instead of making the second crossing of the logging road, turn off the marked trail and follow the road uphill. The mile-long jaunt around the base of Goose Egg Mountain gains about 200 feet.

The Tieton River from Goose Egg Trail

TIETON RIVER

75 LOST LAKE

Skill level intermediate and up
Round trip to Lost Lake 10 miles
Skiing time 6 hours–2 days
Elevation gain 1200 feet
High point 3800 feet
Best January–March
Avalanche potential none
USGS Tieton Basin and
      Foundation Ridge

Map—page 183

Skiing the meadows

Have no fears. Lost Lake is lost no more. In summer a paved road winds up from the valley floor to a small campground by its shores on a broad bench below the fortress-like summits of Divide Ridge. In winter the road becomes a snow-covered avenue through park-like forest of ponderosa pine. A camp at Lost Lake is ideally situated for several days of exploring the many roads and trails that crisscross the area, leading to

many meadows and lakes. (Carry map and compass, however, lest you *do* get lost.)

Drive to the Goose Egg trail (Trail 74) and park, elevation 2550 feet, or turn left on Lost Lake road No. 1402 and continue driving to the snowline.

Elevation is gradually gained on the first mile of the Lost Lake road. The uphill slant then increases but not seriously, remaining moderate all the way. There are few views along the lower section but the lack is not felt; the pure white snow, lush green pine needles, deep orange-red bark, and blue sky more than fill the eye. If that is not enough, after 2½ miles the snow-plastered Bethel Ridge to the north highlights the surroundings. At 4¾ miles a short spur road goes left to the lake and campground, 3800 feet.

For those who don't need to rush back, a loop trip can be done by following the main road to its end and jaunting northeast (towards Divide Ridge) a scant ⅛ mile to Long Lake. After exploring the lake and Pickle Prairie Meadows, just southwest of the road-end, competent routefinders may close the loop by following the Long Lake trail from the north end of the lake back 1 mile to Lost Lake.

For a looping return to the start, at a scant mile below Lost Lake go off on road No. 1402D, rejoining road No. 1402 and thus closing the loop ½ mile from the Goose Egg parking area.

Divide Ridge from Lost Lake road

Mt. Washington from Big Creek road

---

76 BIG CREEK ROAD

Skill level intermediate and up
Round trip up to 14 miles
Skiing time minimum 3 hours
Elevation gain 2700 feet
High point 3600 feet
Best January–March
Avalanche potential moderate
USGS Mt. Steel, The Brothers, and Potlatch

Map—page 186

On a sunny day the scenery can't be beat. Ski Big Creek road for miles as it wanders along slopes of 5944-foot Mt. Ellinor and its next-door neighbor, 6255-foot Mt. Washington. Gaze out over Hood Canal and Puget Sound to Mt. Rainier.

Note: Logging early in 1983 and 1984 may disrupt spring skiing.

From Hoodsport on Highway 101 drive Lake Cushman road 9 miles to the end of pavement, go right 1.5 miles on road No. 24, then left on Big

Creek road No. 2419 to the snowline—wherever that may be as dictated by the mood of the season and the mood of the day.

Since a party won't know in advance how far it can drive, the trip plan must be flexible. Road No. 2419 starts at an elevation of 900 feet and goes nearly 7 miles to end in a clearcut at 3510 feet. It may therefore be a 14-mile day—or much less, depending.

The road sets out from 900 feet in a steady climb for the first 2½ miles, the angle easing off as a spur road is passed. Big Creek is crossed at 3 miles and a long traverse begins along the side of Mt. Washington. At 3½ miles a short spur leads to a clearcut with a broad vista over Lake Cushman and Prospect Ridge. At 3¾ miles pass the Mt. Ellinor trailhead, 3500 feet; the lower stretch of this trail is wooded, narrow, and steep, and the upper portion has avalanche hazard, so skiing is not recommended.

At 4½ miles the road splits. The left fork goes to a clearcut with views down on Lake Cushman; in midwinter, or when snow is unstable, this is a good turnaround-picnic spot, 3600 feet.

For broader views of Puget Sound waterways and cities and Cascade peaks take the right fork (straight ahead), which gains very little elevation as it traverses beneath steep—and avalanche-prone—slopes of Mt. Washington to the Mt. Washington trailhead, another route not recommended for skiing. The road bears eastward along a ridge, rounds a corner, heads north, and at 7 miles ends in a clearcut, 3510 feet.

77 FOUR STREAM ROAD

Skill level intermediate and up
Round trip up to 9 miles to viewpoint
Skiing time 5 hours
Elevation gain up to 1800 feet
High point 3000 feet
Best January–March
Avalanche potential low
USGS Mt. Steel

Map—page 188

Ski from shores of Lake Cushman up through virgin-timber national park and clearcut national forest to a view of the southern Olympics rarely seen except by loggers.

From Hoodsport on Highway 101 drive Lake Cushman road 9 miles to the end of pavement. Turn left along the lakeshore on road No. 24 and

Mt. Lincoln, on the right, from Four Stream road

follow it 5 miles, to near the head of the lake. Go left on Four Stream road No. 2451, which quickly crosses the North Fork Skokomish River, the base point of this trip, elevation 800 feet. Continue driving road No. 2451 to the snowline, which is a mile or two from the river except in periods of unusually deep snow.

Four Stream road climbs steeply and narrowly from the valley floor, blasted from the rocky hillside. At 1½ miles enter Olympic National Park and at 2½ miles leave it at the beginning of a succession of clearcuts. Cross Elk Creek beneath a cliffy shoulder of Lightning Peak. Look northeast to 6154-foot Mt. Pershing, 6255-foot Mt. Washington, Mt. Ellinor, and Copper Mountain.

At 4 miles the road splits. The right fork wanders on for miles through Four Stream drainage. Ski left for the big views. In a scant ½ mile go left to the ridge top and get out the lunch.

Up the North Fork Skokomish, count the valleys on the west side; the valley below you is Four Stream, the next is Five Stream, then Six, Seven, Eight, and Nine, all about a mile apart. North and east are the rugged summits of Mt. Lincoln and Copper Mountain, wearing their white winter overcoats. South is Lightning Peak, its imposing cliffs making it seem much higher than 4654 feet.

Before returning, try a few downhill runs in the clearcuts.

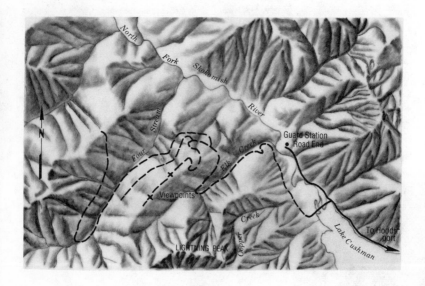

A small stream waiting for the sun to release it from its winter prison

78 MT. TOWNSEND

Skill level basic and up
Round trip to viewpoint 7 miles
Skiing time 4 hours
Elevation gain 600 feet
High point 3900 feet
Best January–March
Avalanche potential low
USGS Tyler Peak

Map—page 190

Steep, rugged terrain and gated roads combine to make winter access to high country of the Olympics nearly impossible. However, at the northern end of the range is one outstanding exception, where open logging roads pass below white ramparts of Mt. Townsend to overlooks of Puget Sound and volcanoes of the Cascades. Trip possibilities are numerous, ranging from half-day tours to overlooks, to a full day or

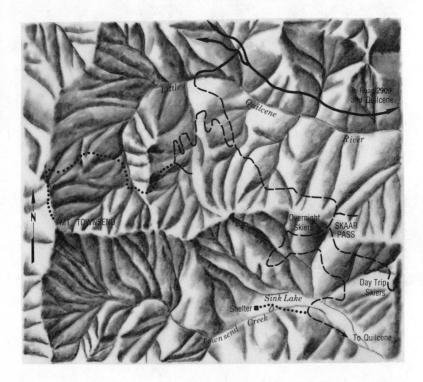

Mt. Townsend

backpack to a little lake, to the very challenging and strenuous ascent of Townsend itself.

Drive Highway 101 north from Quilcene 1.5 miles. Turn left on Lords Lake road 2.9 miles. Just before the lake, turn left on road No. 2909 for 3.6 miles to a major intersection. Take the extreme left fork and head downhill on road No. 2812. In .5 mile is another junction; stay on No. 2812 as it turns right, heading up the Little Quilcene River valley towards Mt. Townsend. The tour starts at the Little Quilcene River bridge, elevation 3025 feet. (After heavy snowfalls be prepared to start skiing sooner —perhaps from Highway 101.)

Cross the bridge and ski 2 miles along clearcut slopes in an ever-growing panorama of the Cascades from Glacier Peak to Mt. Baker. At Skaar Pass, 3700 feet, Mt. Rainier is added to the row of giants.

Day-trippers should take the left spur on the south side of the pass and ski 1 mile, traversing east and then climbing to the summit of a knoll, 3900 feet, for an overlook of Hood Canal and island-dotted Puget Sound.

For longer trips descend from Skaar Pass 1000 feet in 3 miles to Townsend Creek. Follow the Mt. Townsend Trail ½ mile, gaining 150 feet to a small three-sided shelter in the flats of Sink Lake, 2950 feet.

Topnotch skiers may wish to challenge the steep slopes and bowls of Mt. Townsend. At ½ mile past the bridge over the Little Quilcene River turn uphill on an overgrown spur road. Ski around a forested ridge and ascend a clearcut to the top, 4000 feet. Just to the left of the old sparpole landing follow a small creek into dense timber. After 100 yards cross to the right side of the creek and head for a small notch, 4700 feet. On the other side is the first of several basins. Ski northwest into a large forested bowl and good camping. Traverse the bowl and climb a narrow chute that slices through a 200-foot band of rock cliffs. Then follow lightly timbered slopes up to open meadows and the long ridge leading to the summit, 6200 feet.

Steeple Rock and Eagle Point from Hurricane Ridge

79 OBSTRUCTION POINT

WATERHOLE CAMP

Skill level intermediate and up
Round trip 7 miles
Skiing time 5 hours
Elevation gain 200 feet
High point 5000 feet
Best January–April
Avalanche potential low
USGS Mt. Angeles

OBSTRUCTION POINT

Skill level advanced
Round trip 16 miles
Skiing time 2 days
Elevation gain 1300 feet
High point 6200 feet
Best January–April
Avalanche potential low
USGS Mt. Angeles

Map—page 193

The Olympic Mountains have been the victim of bad press in the cross-country world, where stories abound of terrific winter storms and steep terrain. However, a day on Hurricane Ridge, the range's most popular ski area, can put those stories out of mind. The Obstruction

Point Trail avoids the crowds of Hurricane Hill (Trail 80) and leads to excellent skiing in winter beauty and solitude. Day-trippers can enjoy a tour to Waterhole Camp; overnighters can make the panoramic beauty of Obstruction Point their goal.

From Port Angeles drive 17 miles to Hurricane Ridge. Before setting out, register your tour at the Visitor Center. Day skiers can park at the road-end. Overnighters, after registering, must drive back down the road 2½ miles to a parking area, lest their cars be buried by drifting snow in the exposed upper lot.

The Obstruction Point Trail begins, well marked, ½ mile before the day lodge at the last major turn in the highway, elevation 4900 feet. Day-trippers can ski part of the way down from the upper lot to the trailhead, but the last ¼ mile is on a steep slope and it's best to walk the road. Overnighters obviously will drop all packs and most of the party at the trailhead; the driver either can hitch a ride up from the lower lot, usually no problem, or ski the roadside.

In the first ¼ mile the trail drops sharply to the Obstruction Point (summer) road. It then traverses rolling, forested terrain, breaking into the open at 1½ miles on the south side of Steeple Rock. Views extend over the Bailey Range and the Alaskan-looking, 7965-foot lord of the area, Mt. Olympus. In icy snow or bad weather make the edge of the clearing the turnaround.

Beyond the clearing the way reenters forest, traverses two more small hills, and at 3½ miles reaches Waterhole Camp, 5000 feet, a good turn-around for day skiers—keep in mind that the road is gated at dusk.

Overnighters continuing to Obstruction Point face a 900-foot climb in the next ½ mile, passing 6247-foot Eagle Point on its south side. The last 3 miles to Obstruction Point traverse open meadows above the treeline, exposing skiers to grand views, sometimes dangerously icy hills, and perhaps bad weather. The final mile climbs to the end of Obstruction Point road, 6150 feet, with excellent views and campsites. Travel beyond the point is not recommended due to high avalanche potential.

80 HURRICANE HILL

RIDGE ROAD	HILL TOP
Skill level intermediate and up	Skill level advanced
Round trip 3 miles	Round trip 6 miles
Skiing time 2 hours	Skiing time 4 hours
Elevation gain 200 feet	Elevation gain 760 feet
High point 5200 feet	High point 5757 feet
Best January–mid-April	Best January–mid-April
Avalanche potential none	Avalanche potential moderate
USGS Mt. Olympus, Mt. Angeles	USGS Mt. Olympus, Mt. Angeles

Map—page 193

Don't expect to be alone on wide-open, gleaming slopes amid the scenery that in 1982 led the United Nations to designate Olympic National Park a World Heritage Park. In good weather throngs of Nordic skiers swarm the unplowed road from Hurricane Ridge Visitor Center along the rolling ridge towards Hurricane Hill. "Hurricane" is a deserved name and often the road is deeply scooped by wind cirques, so most skiers are content with views over the Elwha River and the Bailey Range from the halfway point.

Snow-plastered trees at the summit of Hurricane Hill

Mt. Olympus, center, from Hurricane Hill

From Port Angeles drive 17 miles to Hurricane Ridge. Register your trip destination at the Visitor Center, elevation 5200 feet.

Ski west from the lodge, skirting the downhill ski area and passing through the snow-play area; watch out for flying innertubes and their screaming pilots who are having the times of their lives. The route follows a summertime road along the ridge descending the first mile, then leveling and climbing a bit to the picnic area at 1½ miles.

A skiers' information board marks the start of the second half, the 1½ miles beyond the road-end to Hurricane Hill. Beyond here, competence in telemark and/or kick-turn are essential. So is an eye for the weather, which in an hour can change from balmy sunshine to blinding blizzards. Be prepared for a quick retreat.

Part of the way is on a very narrow ridge which wind-blown snow gives a knife-edge crest. Stay atop the ridge and climb over a small knoll rather than trying to traverse its very steep and dangerous sides; in unstable or icy conditions this is mandatory. Ski down the far side of the knoll, wary of cornices on the north (right), then around a second knoll to the foot of Hurricane Hill.

A rock outcrop amid stunted, wind-blasted trees marks the summit, 5757 feet. Gaze over Port Angeles, Strait of Juan de Fuca, Victoria, Vancouver Island Mountains, the British Columbia Coast Range, and, of course, Mt. Baker. Reach for another sandwich and turn to gaze over Olympus and the Elwha valley.

On the way back from the picnic area save time to explore open slopes south of the ridge road.

From the right, The Castle, Pinnacle, Plummer, Lane Peaks from Paradise Valley — Trail 67

AND MORE SKI TRAILS

The 80 ski trails covered by this book barely scratch the surface of the skiing opportunities in the Cascades and Olympics. Following is a listing of other places to explore. Unless otherwise noted, these trails are suggested for basic or intermediate skiers.

Nooksack River

Twin Lakes road: Extreme avalanche potential until late spring. 7 miles to lakes and view of Mt. Baker. Park as in Trail 4 and walk highway back to road-maintenance sheds at start of road.

Baker River

Anderson Creek road No. 1107: Steep road, moderate avalanche potential. Ski up to 11 miles each way. Excellent views but difficult when icy. Access: Baker Lake road to mile 13, then follow road No. 1106 across Baker Dam and go right.

Komo Kulshan loop trail: Practice area for basic-level skiers. Access is from Baker Lake road. Park at Nature Trail Sno-Park (Trail 8) and walk back ½ mile to ski trailhead.

Sandy Creek road No. 1124: Up to 14 miles round trip. Good views from clearcuts. Access on Baker Lake road from Nature Trail Sno-Park (Trail 8) or 2 miles farther on at road-end. Some snowmobile use.

Skagit River

Cascade River road: Moderate avalanche potential on this 22-mile-long valley-bottom road. Access from Marblemount. Drive Cascade River road to end of plowing.

Methow River

North Fork Skykomish River road No. 65: Up to 8 miles each way on road to Jack Pass. Views of Monte Cristo peaks and the North Fork valley. Access: North Fork road 9 miles north from Index to end of plowing.

Cutthroat Lake: 1 mile on road followed by 2 miles on trail. Best for advanced skiers. Avalanche potential high all winter. Best to plan trip when the North Cascades Highway is open to trailhead.

Skykomish River

Barclay Creek road No. 6024: 4 miles of road leading to view. Start opposite Baring General Store.

North Fork Skykomish River road No. 65: Up to 8 miles each way on road to Jack Pass. Views of Monte Cristo peaks and the North Fork valley. Access: North Fork road 9 miles north from Index to end of plowing.

Money Creek road: Road tour 7 miles each way to Lake Elizabeth. Valley-bottom trip with views steeply up to peaks of Alpine Lakes Wilderness. Access from Miller River road (Trail 26).

Beckler River road: Road tour, variable length, numerous options on spur roads. Access from Highway 2 east 1 mile from Skykomish.

Wenatchee Lake

Nason Ridge: Long approach on steep trail to rolling, timbered ridge. Best for advanced or mountaineer skiers. Access trail starts opposite entrance to Wenatchee Lake State Park. Alternate approach via Butcher Creek road No. 2717. High avalanche potential west of lookout.

Sears Creek: Over 16 miles of roads, good views and open slopes. May be joined in a loop to the Little Wenatchee River road by overland skiing to meet the Line Creek road system. Access to Sears Creek (Trail 34).

Keechelus Lake

Source Lake–Snow Lake: Extreme avalanche potential. Area not recommended for winter travel.

Commonwealth Basin: High avalanche potential from the edge of timber on up. Not recommended for winter travel.

Stampede Pass: Ski road 6 miles to pass area and many miles to explore beyond with good views and open slopes. Heavy snowmobile use on weekends. Access: Interstate 90 to Sno-Park at Exit 62. Possible site of future Forest Service ski trails. Moderate avalanche potential along road just before Lizard Lake and Pass.

Kachess Lake road: Ski on nearly level road 2 miles to plowed road. Good for beginners. Access: Cabin Creek Exit 63 off Interstate 90.

Cle Elum Lake

Lake Tucquala (Fish Lake): 15-mile road ski to snowbound lake. Heavy snowmobile use. Drive to end of plowed road at Salmon la Sac and ski up main road.

Swauk Creek

Table Mountain: Miles of road and open country to explore. Area receives heavy snowmobile use. Access to Table Mountain (Trail 57).

Mission Ridge to Swauk Pass: 13 miles total. 1½ miles on a ridge top and the remainder on road. Some snowmobile use. Start from upper chair at

Mission Ridge to Haney Meadow, then down to Swauk Pass (Trail 57).

Scotty Creek: 8-mile road ski. Some snowmobile use. Access from the northside Swauk Pass Sno-Park.

White River

Greenwater road: 10 mile road ski to Government Meadows and shelter. Considerable snowmobile use. Access: 2 miles south of town of Greenwater on Highway 410.

West Fork White River: Spring skiing and excellent views from roads and clearcuts of Frog Mountain once West Fork road is open. Access: 3 miles south of Greenwater on Highway 410.

Suntop Lookout: Ski road 6 miles to lookout and views. Extreme avalanche potential on the upper northwest exposed slopes just below

Beaver Pond Trail, Sun Mountain — Trail 14

summit. South-side ascent is recommended. Start same as Grand Park (Trail 58).

Corral Pass road: No parking for this scenic road until spring melt. 4-mile road ski to pass. Access from Highway 410 just north of Silver Spring Lodge.

American River

Blankenship Meadows: Variable-length road ski followed by 3 miles of trail to meadows and lakes below Tumac Mountain for advanced and/or mountaineer skiers. Access from Highway 410. Drive Bumping Lake road to snowline.

Naches River

Nile Creek road: Best for early- or late-season skiing when road is open

Marsh Loops — Trail 47

as far as feed station. Destination and miles variable. Access is from Highway 410 at town of Nile.

Mt. Rainier

Nisqually Vista: ¾-mile round trip on marked trail. Good views of mountain and glacier. Rated easiest by Park Service but very steep in sections. Access: Trail starts behind Paradise Visitor Center.

Sunrise: No parking until park-entrance road has melted out as far as the White River bridge, generally late May or June. Ski 10 miles to end of road then out on open, rolling ridges. Excellent views of Mt. Rainier.

Randle Area

Strawberry Point: Long road ski (25 miles each way) to viewpoint looking into St. Helens' crater. Heavy snowmobile use. Access from Randle via road No. 25 then road No. 2515.

Hamilton Buttes: Advanced spring ski on road and trail over open country. Watch for cornices. Access from Randle. Drive road No. 23, then road No. 21 to road No. 78. At snowline ski onto road No. 7807 past Mud Lake to Buttes Trail.

White Pass

Leech Lake: 3 miles of groomed ski trails on the north side of the pass. Part of the White Pass Ski Area concession, so fee is charged.

Tieton River

Round Mountain road: 4 miles of logging road with few views. Access from Highway 12. Drive west side of Rimrock and Clear lakes to road No. 130.

Road 1430: Basic-level ski on 2 miles of gently rolling road. Access: Ski 300 feet up the Lost Lake road (Trail 75), then turn right.

Olympics

Hamma Hamma River road: Low-elevation valley bottom. As much as 10 miles of skiable road each way. Access from Highway 101 2 miles north of Eldon.

Dosewallips River road: Low-elevation valley-bottom skiing past falls to road-end (5 to 10 miles from snowline). Access off Highway 101 just north of Dosewallips State Park.

Hoh River Trail: Advanced or mountaineer skiers may ski low-elevation valley-bottom trail 8 miles to Olympus Shelter. Trail through rainforest and, if lucky, past herds of elk. Access trail starts at Hoh River Visitor Center.

SUGGESTED READING

AVALANCHE SAFETY

Fraser, Colin. *Avalanches and Snow Safety.* New York: Charles Scribner's Sons, 1978.

LaChapelle, E.R. *The ABC of Avalanche Safety,* 2nd ed. Seattle: The Mountaineers, 1985.

Peters, Ed, ed. *Mountaineering: The Freedom of the Hills.* 4th ed. Seattle: The Mountaineers, 1982.

ENJOYING THE OUTDOORS (Proper clothing, ski equipment, winter camping)

Tejada-Flores, Lito. *Backcountry Skiing.* San Francisco: Sierra Club Books, 1981.

Watters, Ron. *Ski Camping.* San Francisco: Chronicle Books, 1979.

HOW TO

Barnett, Steve. *Cross-Country Downhill.* 2nd ed. Seattle: Pacific Search Press, 1979.

Bein, Vic. *Mountain Skiing.* Seattle: The Mountaineers, 1982.

Gillette, Ned and Dostal, John. *Cross-Country Skiing.* 2nd ed. Seattle: The Mountaineers, 1983.

FIRST AID

Mitchell, Dick. *Mountaineering First Aid.* Seattle: The Mountaineers, 1975.

Wilkerson, James A., M.D., ed. *Medicine for Mountaineering.* 2nd ed. Seattle: The Mountaineers, 1975.

————. *Hypothermia, Frostbite and Other Cold Injuries.* Seattle: The Mountaineers, 1986.

WINTER MOUNTAINEERING IN THE CASCADES

Burgdorfer, Rainer. *Backcountry Skiing in Washington's Cascades.* Seattle, The Mountaineers, 1986.

There are endless possibilities for those who explore

INDEX

Alpine Baldy 82
Alpine Lakes Wilderness . 77, 79
Alta Vista 169
Amabilis Mountain 120
American River 154
Anderson Creek Road 197
Anvil Rock 169
Artist Point 33
Aspen Lake 55
Austin Pass 33

Bagley Lakes 36
Baker, Mt. 24, 30, 36
Baker Hot Springs 40
Baker Ski Area, Mt. 33,36
Baker Trail, Mt. 24
Bald Mountain 158
Bald Mountain Road 27
Bandera Overlook 104
Bar Creek 30
Barclay Creek Road 197
Barlow Pass 74
Barometer Mountain 30
Bear Gap 150
Bearpaw Mountain 27
Beaver Creek Road 51
Beckler Peak Road 82
Beckler River Road 198
Benton Creek Road 157
Bessemer-Green Ridge 103
Bessemer Mountain 102
Bessemer Mountain, South . 103
Big Creek Road 185
Big Four Ice Caves 74
Big Four Picnic Area 73, 75
Blankenship Meadows . 180, 200
Blewett Pass 138, 144
Boulder Creek 39
Bowen Mountain 51
Buck Mountain 48
Buesch Lake 180
Bullion Basin 148
Burley Mountain 170

Cabin Creek 122

Camp Lake 135
Camp Muir 167
Camp Robber Creek 78
Campbell Lake 51
Campground Loops 142
Canteen Flats 158
Canyon Creek Road 26
Canyon Ridge Trail 28
Cascade River Road 197
Castle Peak 163
Castle Ranch Loop 43
Castle Saddle 163
Catherine Loop,
  Mt. 108, 111
Chinook Pass 152
Chiwaukum Mountains . . 88, 90
Cle Elum River 127, 128
Cleman Mountain 158
Coal Creek 74
Coal Lake 75
Coal Lake Road 74
Cold Creek Trail 108, 110
Coleman Glacier Overlook . . 25
Commonwealth Basin 198
Cooper Lake 133
Cooper Pass 133
Cooper River Road 129, 132
Corral Pass Road 200
Cougar Divide 29
Cougar Lake 51
Cougar Mountain 48
Coulter Ski Trail 88, 91
Cowlitz Pass 178
Crown Point 149
Crystal Mountain
  Ski Area 148, 150
Cub Creek 47
Cut-Off Trail 53
Cutthroat Lake 197

Damfino Lakes 28
Dead Horse Lake 55
Deer Creek Pass 66, 71
Deer Creek Road 70, 72
Deer Lake 179

Dewey Lakes 152
Diamond Head 145
Diamond T Ranch 46
Dillard Point 37
Diving Hawk Ski Trail 53
Dorothy, Lake 77
Dosewallips River Road 201
Double Eagle Road 71, 72

Eagle Point 193
Easton Trail, Lake 122
Elbow Coulee Road 55
Eleanor Creek 147
Eleanor, Lake 148
Elizabeth, Lake 198
Elk Creek 188
Ellinor Trail, Mt. 186
Excelsior Mountain Trail 27

Fawn Peak 48
Finney Creek Road 41
Finney Peak 43
Fish Hatchery Trail 101
Fish Lake 198
Flying Loop 97
Foss River 79
Foss River Trail, East Fork . . . 80
Foss River Trail, West Fork . . 81
Four Stream Road 187
French Cabin Creek 126, 128
French Cabin Mountain 128
Frog Mountain 199

Gee Point Road 43
Glacier Vista 167
Goat Creek 48
Goat Rocks Wilderness 172
Gold Creek Valley 113, 115
Golf Course Loops 101
Goose Egg Mountain 182
Goose Egg Trail 181
Government Meadows 199
Grand Park 146
Green Mountain 60
Greenwater Road 199

Hamilton Buttes 201
Hamma Hamma River
    Road 201

Haney Meadow Trail . . . 141, 144
Hannegan Road 31
Hansen Creek 106
Heather Lake Trail 69
Heather Ridge 84
Heliotrope Ridge 24
Hells Crossing
    Campground 154
Hen Skin Lake 151
Herman Saddle 35
Hidden Valley Trail 109, 111
Hogback Mountain 177
Hoh River Trail 201
Huckleberry Creek Road 147
Hurricane Hill 194
Hurricane Ridge 192
Hyak 108, 110
Hyak Lake 110
Hyak, Mt. 110

Independence Lake 76

Jack Pass 198
Jim Hill Mountain 88
Jolly Road 131
Jolly Too Road 131
Julius, Lake 91
Jungle Creek 135

Kachess Lake Road 117, 198
Kachess Lake, South 124
Kelcema Lake 71
Kendall Knob 114
Kendall Peak Lakes 114
Kendall Peak Road 112, 116
Kidney Creek Road 27
Knox Creek 127
Komo Kulshan Loop Trail . . . 197
Kulshan Cabin 25
Kulshan Ridge 34

Lake Creek Trail, Upper 172
Lake Easton State Park 122
Lanham Creek 88
Lanham Lake 87
Leavenworth 99
Leavenworth Ski Hill
    Loop 101
Leech Lake 179, 201

Leonards Ridge 43
Lillian, Mt. 145
Lion Rock 145
Little Quilcene River 191
Lizard Lake 198
Loch Eileen 91
Long Lake 184
Lost Lake 183
Louise Lake 161
Loup-Loup 56

Maloney Ridge 81
Margaret, Mt. 117
Marsh Loops 124
Martin Lake-Morovitz Loop . . 39
Martin Lake Road 39
Mason Lake Way 105
Mazama Dome 36
Mazama Ridge 161, 165
McClure Rock 169
McCue Ridge 92
McDonald, Lake 92
McWaukum Braes 92
Meadow Creek 160
Medicine Creek Road 137
Methow River 44
Methow Valley Ski Touring
    Association 43, 46, 55
Methow Valley Trail 54
Midway Camp 89
Mill Creek 87, 110
Miller River 77
Miller River, West Fork 77
Mission Ridge
    Ski Area 145, 198
Money Creek Road 198
Mountain Holm 124
Mountain Loop
    Highway 73, 75
Mowich Lake 159

Naches Peak 152
Naneum Meadows, Upper . . 145
Narada Falls 161, 163
Nason Ridge 198
Nile Creek Road 200
Nisqually Vista 201
No Name Ridge 133
Nomad Ski Camp 89, 91

Nooksack Cirque Trail 32
Nooksack Falls 30
Nooksack River Road,
    North Fork 31
Nordic Pass 109
Norse Peak 149
North Cascades Highway . . . 197
North Lookout Road 63
North Mountain 63, 127

Obstruction Point 192
Olallie Meadows 109, 111
Olympic National
    Park 188, 192, 194, 201
Owhi Campground 133

Pacific Crest Trail 87, 178
Pacific West Ski
    Resort 108, 110
Packwood Lake 172
Panorama Point 167
Paradise 165, 167
Paradise Valley Road . . 161, 165
Park Butte 36
Park Creek 40
Pass Lake 76
Patterson Lake 55
Pauls Peak Picnic Area 159
Pebble Creek 169
Perry Creek 74
Pete Lake 133
Pickle Prairie Meadows 184
Pigtail Peak 177
Pilchuck Mountain Road 67
Pinnacle Peak 164
Pipeline Road 172
Pipestone Canyon 50
Pleasant Valley
    Campground 154
Pleasant Valley Loop 154
Poal Patch Campground . . . 171
Pressentin Watershed 43

Rainbow Falls 40
Rainier National Park, Mt. . . 125,
    146, 159, 161, 163, 165, 167,
    200
Red Top Lookout 136

Red Top Mountain
  Lookover 136
Reflection Lakes . .161, 163, 165
Reflection Lakes
  Cutoff Trail 161, 166
Rendevous Cabin 48
Rendevous Pass. 46
Road 1430 201
Roaring Creek 91
Rockdale Lake 109
Rocky Creek Ski Trail 38
Rocky Prairie. 156
Round Mountain Road 201
Ruth Creek 31
Rye Creek Road 135

Sand Lake 178
Sandy Creek Road 197
Sawyer Mountain 79
Sawyer Pass. 79
Schreibers Meadow 38
Scottish Lakes 88, 90
Scotty Creek Road 144, 199
Sears Creek 96, 198
Segelsen Creek Road 64
Segelsen Ridge Road 66
Shadow of Sentinels
  Nature Trail 38, 39
Silver Basin 150
Sink Lake 191
Skaar Pass 191
Skykomish River Road,
  North Fork 198
Skyline Lake 85
Sno-Park 18, 31, 38, 39, 56,
    59, 87, 97, 104, 112, 115, 117,
    120, 122, 141, 143, 145
Snoqualmie Pass . . 108, 110, 112,
    115, 117
Snow Lake 198
Soaring Hawk 53
Sobieski Mountain 81
Source Lake 198
South Summit Road 56
Stampede Pass. 198
Steeple Rock 193
Stevens Canyon Road . . 161, 163

Stillaguamish River,
  North Fork. 64
Stillaguamish River,
  South Fork 73
Strawberry Point 201
Sugar Loaf 169
Sulphur Creek Cutoff Trail . .38
Summer Trail 92
Sun Mountain 52
Sunrise 201
Sunrise Mine Road 74
Suntop Lookout 199
Susan Jane, Lake 88
Swauk Pass Meadow
  Loop 141, 145
Swauk Pass 141, 143, 144,
  198, 199
Swede Heaven Road 65

Table Mountain
  Road 34, 35, 142, 144, 198
Tatoosh Range 162, 163
Teanaway Butte 134
Telemark Mountain 58
Texas Pond 63
Thompson Ridge Road 53
Thorp Creek Trail 126
Thorp Lake 127
Thorp Mountain 127
Three Forks Junction . . . 109, 110
Three Forks Trail 109, 110
Tieton River. 181
Tipsoo Lake 153
Tired Creek 133
Tonga Ridge 79
Townsend Creek 191
Townsend Trail, Mt. 191
Townsend, Mt. 190
Trollhaugen Hut 120
Tronsen Campground 142
Tronsen Meadow Trail .142, 145
Tucquala, Lake 198
Tumac Mountain 180, 200
Twin Lakes Road. 197
Twin Lakes Trail 108

Upper Pine Forest Trail 53

Washington Trail, Mt. 186
Waterhole Camp 192
Wells Creek 29
Wenatchee State Park,
    Lake 93
Wenatchee Ridge 143
Whistler Creek Road 27

White Pass . . . 174, 177, 178, 201
White River, West Fork 199
White River Road 95
White River Viewpoint 95
Windy Pass 109

Yellow Jacket Road 174

Write for illustrated catalog of more than 100 outdoor titles:
The Mountaineers • Books
306 Second Avenue West, Seattle WA 98119